Toward a Grammar
of Curriculum Practice

Toward a Grammar of Curriculum Practice

Embracing New Conceptions of Curriculum and Curriculum Planning

EDMUND C. SHORT

Published by State University of New York Press, Albany

© 2023 State University of New York

All rights reserved

Printed in the United States of America

No part of this book may be used or reproduced in any manner whatsoever without written permission. No part of this book may be stored in a retrieval system or transmitted in any form or by any means including electronic, electrostatic, magnetic tape, mechanical, photocopying, recording, or otherwise without the prior permission in writing of the publisher.

For information, contact State University of New York Press, Albany, NY
www.sunypress.edu

Library of Congress Cataloging-in-Publication Data

Name: Short, Edmund C., author.
Title: Toward a grammar of curriculum practice : embracing new
 conceptions of curriculum and curriculum planning / Edmund C. Short.
Description: Albany : State University of New York Press, [2023] |
 Includes bibliographical references and index.
Identifiers: ISBN 9781438493466 (hardcover : alk. paper) | ISBN
 9781438493480 (ebook) | ISBN 9781438493473 (pbk. : alk. paper)
Further information is available at the Library of Congress.

10 9 8 7 6 5 4 3 2 1

Contents

Illustrations	vii
Preface	ix
Introduction	1
Chapter 1 How Practice Is to Be Defined	5
Chapter 2 How Curriculum Is to Be Defined Constituent Components of a Curriculum	15 28

Chapter 3
How Curriculum Practice Is to Be Defined
    Deliberations
    Preferred Conceptions and Actions
    Prescriptions
	47
	63
	72
	76

Chapter 4
How a Grammar of Curriculum Practice Is to Be Conceptualized
    Semantic Analysis and Construction of Individual Directives
    The Meaningful Structure of a Combined Set of Directives
	87
	
	94
	
	96

Chapter 5
The Value and Use of a Grammar of Curriculum Practice   105

Chapter 6
What This Book Has Attempted to Do   115

Closing Summary   119

Notes   121

References   129

Index   145

About the Author   149

Illustrations

Figure

2.1	Web of curriculum components.	43

Tables

1.1	Perspectives on Practice	10
2.1	Conceptualizations of the Domain of Curriculum	23
2.2	Curriculum Components	26
2.3	Authors Identifying Curriculum Components by Category	27
2.4	Ten Essential Components of Curriculum	41
3.1	Classifications of Conceptions of Curriculum Practice	55
3.2	Categories of Actions within Deliberation	67
3.3	Illustrative Directives in the Ten Components of Curriculum	80
4.1	A Grammar of Curriculum Practice	100

Boxes

I.1	Scholars Advocating Curriculum Work as a Practice	3
1.1	Definitions of *Practice* in the General Literature of Professional Practice	6
1.2	Definitions of *Practice* by Scholars in the Field of Curriculum	7
2.1	Definitions of *Curriculum* by Curriculum Textbook Writers and Scholars	16
2.2	Analytic Work Done to Distinguish Sometimes Overlapping Concepts Related to Curriculum	20
3.1	Textbooks Explaining How Curriculum Development Can Be Conceptualized	49
3.2	Key Concepts in Curriculum Work as Perceived by Curriculum Experts	49
3.3	Key Concepts in Curriculum Work Derived from Empirical Studies	53
3.4	Descriptions of Deliberation by Various Curriculum Experts	64
3.5	Advantages of Adopting the Stipulated Definition of Curriculum Practice	85
4.1	Collected Definitions of Constituent Concepts in a Grammar of Curriculum Practice	102
5.1	Highlights of this Conceptualization of a Grammar of Curriculum Practice	112

Preface

This book makes the case for a new way of conceiving the activities of curriculum planning. It presents a detailed argument for adopting specific concepts for structuring this work that are intended to overcome perceived problems associated with traditional conceptualizations of curriculum planning. Redefined are conceptions of what constitutes a curriculum, how to determine what is to be prescribed for every component of a curriculum, and how such prescriptions shall be stated and interrelated. Key concepts elucidated within this new conceptualization include (1) curriculum deliberation, (2) curriculum prescriptions, (3) curriculum directives, and (4) curriculum practice, among others. The full array of concepts defined in this book, and the particular way they are structured, constitutes a grammar of curriculum practice meant to facilitate thinking about and doing curriculum planning in Pre-K–12 education. The argument presented here employs the techniques of conceptual analysis and construction.

Introduction

What do curriculum practitioners do? How is their work to be conceived and enacted? Do existing formulations of this work adequately express and meaningfully communicate what is to be done and how to do it? How flexible and adaptable are these formulations in differing settings and circumstances? Is one universal conception of this work desirable or not? These and other related questions form the impetus for a search for a grammar of curriculum practice.

This book addresses the discourses and practices enacted by curriculum practitioners. It undertakes systematic reflection on the distinctive words and discourses and the distinctive deeds and practices employed by curriculum practitioners. Its aim is to formulate an outline of a grammar of curriculum discourse and practice that facilitates understanding and communication among curriculum practitioners and others concerned with their work. The emphasis is on analyzing and clarifying the language of curriculum discourse and practice and on identifying generic structures that underlie the variety of terminology and meanings that surface in ordinary instances of curriculum discourse and practice. Such a grammar constitutes the fundamental structure of curriculum practice on which particular formulations of curriculum discourses, doctrines, actions, and practices can be articulated and acted on. Such a grammar becomes the basis for teaching and learning how to speak about and enact the work that curriculum practitioners do.[1]

I choose to refer to the people who do curriculum work as *curriculum practitioners*. While this is not a term commonly given to those who do such work, it is deliberately chosen as a starting point in this effort to create a grammar of curriculum practice as a way to begin to conceive of this work in a new light. Curriculum work has traditionally been referred to as curriculum development, curriculum planning, curriculum making, curriculum designing, curriculum coordinating, curriculum supervision, curriculum management, curriculum negotiating, or using other similar terms. Those who lead this kind of curriculum work have traditionally been called curriculum specialists, curriculum developers, curriculum coordinators, and so on. Terminology of this kind has typically been so ill-defined that curriculum work has been conceived very imprecisely and without much agreement as to what is entailed in doing this work. A new way of conceiving the work of curriculum practitioners is clearly needed.

To label those who do curriculum work as *curriculum practitioners* is to construe their work as a form of professional practice, adopting the language found in the scholarly writings of authors such as Parsons (1968), Schwyzer (1969), Argyris and Schon (1974), MacIntyre (1984), Schatzki (2001, 2012, 2018), Polkinghorne (2004), Schwandt (2005), Green (2009), Kemmis (2010, 2014), Billett et al. (2014), and Mahon et al. (2017). There is precedent for using the language of practice in connection with curriculum work, although it has not been widely adopted or exploited. A number of curriculum scholars have advocated conceiving of curriculum work as a practice. (See box I.1.)

Although these curriculum scholars have consistently observed over several decades that curriculum can be, and for compelling reasons should be, viewed as a practice, this way of conceiving of curriculum work has not become common or very influential in either the conduct of ordinary curriculum activities or in the field of curriculum scholarship.

By contrast, of the two central domains of education—curriculum and teaching—it is the work of teaching that has

Box I.1
Scholars Advocating Curriculum Work as a Practice

Schwab, 1969; Walker, 1971; Westbury, 1972; Connelly, 1974; Pring, 1975/2004; Stenhouse, 1975; Reid, 1978/2013, 1999; Goodlad, 1979; Wise, 1979; Schubert, 1980, 1986; Short, 1983, 1991; Vallance, 1983; Harris, 1985; Yinger, 1987; Connelly & Clandinin, 1988; Walker, 1992; Kemmis, 1995; McCutcheon, 1995; van den Akker 2003, 2013; Walker, 2003; Sears, 2004; Wraga, 2006; Connelly, He, & Phillion, 2008; Dillon, 2009; Gaztambide-Feranadez & Theissen, 2009; Whitson, 2009; Connelly & Xu, 2010; Grimmett & Halvorson, 2010; Connelly & Xu, 2012; Uljens & Ylimaki, 2017; Deng, 2018; Ruzgar, 2018.

been persistently treated as a professional practice and has been more thoroughly studied as a practice than has curriculum work. Teaching has long been construed as a professional practice (e.g., Jackson, 1980; van Manen, 1999; Danielson, 2007; Gitomer & Bell, 2016); so it is surprising that curriculum work has not similarly been understood to be a professional practice. One reason may be because the term *practice* is often taken to mean something performed by an individual and not by groups of people. Unlike teaching practice, which is ordinarily undertaken by an individual teacher, curriculum practice is usually undertaken by a group of individuals collaborating with one another. Curriculum practice is a collective enterprise similar to that undertaken in practices such as producing theater or mining or legislating, and differs from practices such as accounting or surgery or acting that are carried out by individuals. Both of these conceptions of practice are acceptable, as these examples from other fields of practice affirm. Curriculum work should not be excluded from being considered a practice because it involves groups of people.

Whether to call curriculum work a practice, or whether any kind of professional activity should be called a practice, hinges on what definition is given to the term *practice*. So it is with the problem of defining *practice* that we begin the task of creating a grammar of curriculum practice. Attention to defining and elucidating the other key terms included in this topic—*curriculum, curriculum practice,* and *grammar*—will follow.

Chapter 1

How Practice Is to Be Defined

First of all, we are not concerned here with the occupational definition of practice, that is, with work viewed as labor or as an economic enterprise, nor with its status or value as a social institution among other social institutions. Rather, the focus to be assumed here is on what those engaged in the practice say and do in the course of their work, on their discourse and actions, on their activity. Taking this stance on a definition of practice permits us to identify language and structure that will be useful to practitioners in the actual conduct of their practice. The kinds of thinking, speaking, and doing that constitute the essential features of actual practice (curriculum practice, in this instance) are the dimensions of practice that should be compatible with the definition of practice we adopt. Since the focus in this book is on curriculum practice, questions about what counts as curriculum practice, its essential order and structure, its most viable concepts, its characteristic discourse and activities, in a word—its grammar—requires that we adopt a definition of practice that can encompass these questions. Standard dictionaries offer such nontechnical definitions of practice as: "the action or process of performing or doing something," "something usually or regularly or customarily done," "the actual performance or an activity in a real situation," "a way of doing something," "the act of doing something"—where practice is used as a noun (we are not interested in its use as a verb, as in "repeatedly practicing something").

The general literature on professional practice offers a number of more nuanced definitions of practice. (See box 1.1 for a list of quoted definitions of practice by several scholars of professional practice.) Other scholars have given definitions of practice more specific to the work of curriculum practice. (See box 1.2 for a list of quoted definitions of practice by several scholars in the field of curriculum.)

Box 1.1
Definitions of *Practice* in the General Literature of Professional Practice

"By a 'practice' I mean any coherent and complex form of socially established cooperative human activity through which goods internal to that form of activity are realised in the course of trying to achieve those standards of excellence which are appropriate to, and partly definitive of, that form of activity, with the result that human powers to achieve excellence, and human conceptions of the ends and goods involved, are systematically extended" (MacIntyre, 1984, 175).

"A practice is a repeatable human action that stands in a communal tradition of identification and description" (Jones, 2002, 15).

"Practice is a complex set of techniques that can be considered, changed, deployed, taught, learned, and transferred independently of the contingent and temporal circumstances of actual situated practice" (Schwandt, 2005, 316).

"Practices are about taking the right action in consideration of this situation, this person, at this time and place, in this set of circumstances. . . . They are fluid, changeable, dynamic, and are characterized by their alterability, indeterminacy, and particularity. . . . They employ deliberation, uncertainty, wise judgment, and are situated, contingent, and socially enacted" (Schwandt, 2005, 322, 323).

"Practice is what particular people do in a particular place and time, employing learned capacities and competencies, and involving identity work and emotional work" (Kemmis, 2010, 143, elaborated in fig. 8.3).

"A practice is an open-ended, spatially-temporally dispersed nexus of doings and sayings" (Schatski, 2012, 14).

"A practice is a form of socially established cooperative human activity in which characteristic arrangements of actions and activities (doings) are comprehensible in terms of arrangements of relevant ideas in characteristic discourses (sayings), and when the people and objects involved are distributed in characteristic arrangements of relationships (relatings), and when this complex of sayings, doings and relatings 'hangs together' in a distinctive project" (Kemmis et al., 2014, 31).

Box 1.2
Definitions of *Practice* by Scholars in the Field of Curriculum

"Curriculum development is essentially the result of cooperative effort and by its very nature must draw upon many kinds of competencies" (Herrick, 1950, 37).

"The main operations in curriculum deliberation are formulating decision points, devising alternative choices at these decision points, considering arguments for and against suggested alternatives, and choosing the most defensible alternative subject to acknowledged constraints" (Walker, 1971, 54).

"[The curriculum] practitioner can be considered a designer of educational environments . . . so that events flow in valued ways . . . [as a result of] reaching agreements involving people with different values and intentions . . . [both an esthetic and a political design problem]" (Huebner, 1975, 266).

"The activity of constructing a curriculum is a purposive set of actions—a telic pattern . . . All curriculum talk and work is value based" [Macdonald, 1977, 18, 21).

"The [curriculum] developer works with some vision of a better set of learning activities for students . . . The developer must sharpen this vision and articulate its rationale, embody the vision in materials or instructions that others can use, identify the requirements for their effective use, and persuade others of the value of the design" (Wise, 1979, 22).

"[Curriculum practice] requires a group . . . for the identification of the places where change is wanting, the borrowing or invention of alternative ways of fulfilling identified wants, and the deliberation on the costs and benefits of these alternatives" (Schwab, 1983, 244).

"Curriculum practice is defined as all those practical activities concerned with conceiving, expressing, justifying, and enacting educational programs" (Short, 1991, 359).

"I take curriculum to be a field of practice. . . . Curriculum work is concerned with services and problems related to the purposes and content of the educational program of the school and how these are organized in time, in relation to one another, and in relation to the people involved and to the physical and social milieu" (Walker, 1992, 109).

"If someone asks what curriculum specialists do, it is possible to respond by saying that their responsibilities extend from the shaping of educational policy bearing on the aims and content of educational programs to work dealing with the design of specific elements within particular educational programs. . . . Curriculum development is the process of transforming images and aspirations about education into programs that will effectively realize the visions that initiated the process" (Eisner, 2002, 31, 126).

"We define curriculum practice as the process of formulating aims and selecting contents and reflecting methods, including pedagogical experiences through which content is enacted . . . These processes are dialogical and discursively constructed" (Uljens & Ylimaki, 2017, 39–40).

On close examination, it is evident that the authors of these many definitions of practice, whether intended to be all-encompassing or to focus only on the work of curriculum practitioners, do not agree on what practice is and how it should be defined. Each definition reflects a certain perspective from which its author is viewing practice. Is there a proper perspective that should be taken when defining practice? If so, which perspective is to be adopted? Which definition, or what other definition, is an appropriate one to use in conceptualizing curriculum practice and in creating a grammar of it? To assist in deciding on an appropriate definition of practice to use for this purpose, it will be helpful to do an analysis of some of the perspectives that have been taken or can be taken on defining practice.

Table 1.1 presents several possible perspectives on practice, identifies certain key concepts employed in each of these perspectives, cites seminal sources for each, and lists sources by curriculum scholars who have worked within each of these perspectives. Each of the definitions of practice quoted in boxes 1.1 and 1.2 has drawn on one or more of these perspectives. For instance, MacIntyre's definition (1984) is both sociological and moral/ethical in its perspective. Jones's definition (2002) probably relates to the moral/ethical perspective. Schwandt's definitions (2005) have aspects of the praxeological/procedural, the moral/ethical, and the naturalistic/operational perspectives. Schatski's (2012) and Kemmis's (2010, 2018) definitions exhibit features of the naturalistic/operational and the sociological perspectives. Herrick's definition (1950) combines the epistemic, the sociological, and the technological perspectives. Walker's (1971) clearly falls within the naturalistic/operational perspective. Both the technological and the naturalistic/operational perspectives appear to be evident in Huebner's (1975) definition. Macdonald's (1977) definition embraces the sociological, the moral/ethical, and the phenomenological/hermeneutical perspectives. Wise's (1979) has elements of multiple perspectives: praxeological/procedural, technological, naturalistic/operational, moral/

Table 1.1. Perspectives on Practice

Perspective	Concepts Employed	Seminal Sources	Sources by Curriculum Scholars
General Systems	Interacting Social Systems	Bertalanffy, 1968; Skyttner, 2005	Beauchamp, 1961/1981; Faix, 1964
Sociological	Roles and Functions	Parsons & Shils, 1951	Goodlad, 1979; Kemmis, 2009
Moral/Ethical	Standards of Goodness/Professionalism	MacIntyre, 1984; Carr, 2014	Macdonald & Purpel, 1987
Praxeological/Procedural	Rules/Procedures for Efficient Action	Kotarbinski, 1965	Tyler, 1949; Taba, 1962; Iwanska, 1979
Technological	Design/Development Strategies Tested until Goal Achieved	Nadler, 1981	van den Akker, 2003
Epistemic	Knowledge Acquisition and Use	Markauskaite & Goodyear, 2014	Clandinin, 1985; Connelly & Clandidin, 1985
Phenomenological/Hermeneutical	Perceived Meanings	Heidegger, 1982; van Manen, 1997; 2007; 2014	Polakow, 1986; Berman et al, 1991

Aesthetic	Creative Combination of Elements into Pleasing Qualities of Form or Narrative	Parker, 1926; Phenix, 1964; Mitchell, 1981; Polkinghorne, 1988	Connelly & Clandinin, 1988; Eisner, 1998
Naturalistic/ Operational	Situation Specific/ Deliberative/ Rhetorical/Temporal Agreement	McKeon, 1952; Raup et al., 1962	Schwab, 1969; Walker, 1971; Uljens & Ylimaki, 2017

ethical, and philosophical/analytical. Schwab's (1983) definition is primarily naturalistic/operational, with an epistemic perspective also evident. Short's (1991) definition of practice includes the sociological and the naturalistic/operational perspectives. Walker's (1992) is naturalistic/operational and technological. Eisner's (2002) is sociological, praxeological/procedural, and technological. Uljens and Ylimaki's (2017) definition of practice is technological and naturalistic/operational.[1]

One of the problems with adopting any one, or a mix, of these perspectives is that almost all of them assume that practice should be addressed from the outside and seek to discover generalizations *about* practice (and that this will facilitate practice), rather than conceive of practice as a phenomenon that proceeds without benefit of generalizations *about* it and has its own internal logic governed by the nature of the activity itself. The perspectives toward the end of table 1.1 tend to support this latter conceptualization; the naturalistic/operational perspective seems to be the one most nearly consistent with this view of practice. For this reason, I choose to adopt a definition of practice that adheres to the *naturalistic/operational perspective*, where the definition specifies concepts embracing what actually goes on during the conduct of practice in real situations. This type of definition is one that can directly communicate what is to be done in actual practice.

Therefore, stated in the most general terms, I define a practice as *a series of sayings and doings undertaken by a person or persons to accomplish an intended purpose in a given domain of socially valued activity*. This definition is quite similar to the one stated by Kemmis et al. (2014) in box1.1. Such a definition takes on precise meaning only as it is associated with a particular practice in which the purpose is clearly stated and the nature of its inherent work is clearly identified. This will be the goal of attempting to define "curriculum practice" in a chapter 2 of this book.

Meanwhile, some commentary may be helpful in seeing the wisdom of choosing to define practice in this particular way. Regarding the point made about the inappropriateness of defining practice from the perspectives taken by many scholars of practice (in table 1.1), their work has been primarily intended to *describe* practice using theoretical frameworks suitable for seeing particular aspects of practice, none of which portray the practice holistically. For instance, describing or explaining sociologically the "roles and functions" that people perform in practice, while these features of practice certainly do exist, does not get at the heart of what is done in a practice and clearly not the whole of it. In another instance, trying out "design strategies" to develop a technological product until a proven process is found may or may not be part of what goes on in a practice, but again this is not the whole of it. Doing "meaningful or qualitatively pleasing activities" may be features of a practice, but these surely do not fully define the practice. What is called for in an adequate definition of practice is some conception of the distinguishing features operating in a given instance of performing the practice in toto and in situ, undivided analytically for purposes of description or for some other reason.

Regarding my specifying that "sayings and doings" are the key elements in a definition of practice, I have come to this conclusion as a result of observing the arguments of scholars of practice such as Schatzki (2012) and Kemmis et al. (2014), mentioned previously. Schatzki (2012), in an article titled, "A Primer on Practices," argues that "a practice is a nexus of doings and sayings. . . . At the base of a practice lie those doings and sayings that are basic activities. Basic activities take place without the actor having to do something else: they are actions a person can perform without further ado" (15). He further states that "practices are instituted when activities come to be organized by some set of understandings, rules, and teleoaffective structure. . . . To effect such an organization, tasks must be distributed, ends and purposes set or coalesced, and rules issued or disseminated" (23). He also asserts that "language is an important clue as to which activities and practices exist. . . . The use of words for activities and practices is built into practices" (24).

Kemmis et al. (2014), as noted above, argue in quite elaborate ways (and much like Schatzki does) that a practice consists of arrangements of doings, sayings, and relatings. Elsewhere, Mahon et al. (2017) restate this definition of practice more succinctly: A practice is "a socially established cooperative human activity involving utterances and forms of understanding (sayings), modes of action (doings), and ways in which people relate to one another and the world (relatings) that 'hang together' in characteristic ways in a distinctive 'project'" (24, table 1.1). This understanding of practice not only embraces a holistic view of it, but it also identifies just three key concepts as essential for recognizing and participating in a practice, thereby providing clear direction for specifying the most basic kinds of activity that are to be engaged in. When fleshed out for particular practices, this definition would allow one to distinguish one sort of practice from any other by showing how the sayings, doings, and relatings differ in each case. I find this structure appealing for the purpose of stipulating a general definition of practice, as well as serving as a basis for adopting an appropriate one for curriculum practice, because of its precision and its grounding in the realities of actual practice rather than in the limited usefulness of theoretical understandings (see Bourdieu [1977] and Polkinghorne [2004]). So, on the basis of the arguments of Schatzki and Kemmis, I have been persuaded to adopt as a definition of practice, presented in its simplest form, the statement asserted above, that a practice is *a series of sayings and doings undertaken by a person or persons to accomplish an intended purpose in a given domain of socially valued activity.*

Chapter 2

How Curriculum Is to Be Defined

The place to begin in this endeavor to generate a grammar of curriculum practice is with its central term—*curriculum*. What do we mean by this term? To what do we refer when we attach the name *curriculum* to some phenomenon? Exactly what phenomenon are we rightly able to call a curriculum and not confuse it with some other perhaps closely related phenomenon? How do we know when we "see" one? What constitutes curriculum in a generic sense rather than in the sense of particular examples? These and related questions must be addressed if we are to link the term *curriculum* to something called curriculum practice.

The existing scholarly work germane to answering these questions tends to be focused on the many definitions and descriptions of curriculum that have accumulated over time (most of which are contested). The term *curriculum* indeed has a wide variety of referents in common usage. As a first cut, by way of limiting the definition to be sought in this book on a grammar of curriculum practice, it will refer only to what generally is understood to be an educational program authorized and supported by some educational institution. It need not have legal standing and may be informal in its sponsorship. However, for purposes of the treatment to be given here, *curriculum* will refer exclusively to precollegiate educational programs, in recognition of the fact it is often used quite differently in higher education.

Curriculum at precollegiate levels of education has been described informally by expressions such as "all the experiences under the guidance of the school," "a planned course of study," "the content to be taught," "a student's required sequence of studies," "a set of instructional units," "a set of objectives to be achieved," "a structured series of learning outcomes," "a set of intended learnings," "a document produced by curriculum planners or developers," and "specifications for teaching and learning." Needless to say, curriculum practitioners, those who are entrusted to put together a curriculum, find these informal definitions of what a curriculum is to be less than helpful in doing their work. First of all, which definition is to be followed? Precisely what is entailed in putting together a curriculum defined in any of these ways? What things must be decided on and what form should those decisions take? A more specific and revealing definition of curriculum is needed. All kinds of attempts to define curriculum more precisely and more helpfully have been undertaken by curriculum textbook writers and other curriculum scholars. (See a few of them quoted in box 2.1.)

Box 2.1
Definitions of Curriculum by
Curriculum Textbook Writers and Scholars

"[Curriculum phenomena are defined as] the universe of planned and unplanned activities and events resulting from the interaction of the variables in an instructional program" (Faix, 1964, 8).

"[Curriculum is to be conceived as] a design of educative environments in which valued educational activity can occur; [where] past traditions, collective memories, and artifacts [are brought] into the presence of the young for their active thought and response" (Huebner, 1966, 94; 1974, 41–42).

"Curriculum consists of certain component elements. It includes some notion of the nature of content; it provides for categories of instruction; and it ordinarily includes reference to modes of teaching" (Broudy, Smith, & Burnett, 1966, 74).

"Curriculum is a set of events, either proposed, occurring, or having occurred, which has the potential for restructuring human experience. It has structural, process, and value dimensions" (Duncan & Frymier, 1967, 183).

"A curriculum is an attempt to communicate the essential principles and features of an educational proposal in such a form that it is open to critical scrutiny and capable of effective translation into practice" (Stenhouse, 1975, 4).

"[The term] curriculum is used when reference is made to a set of values, skills, and beliefs which are available in a particular environment to be learned" (Derr, 1977, 152).

"The term curriculum (a) is used to refer to an intentionally promulgated set of rules the purpose of which is to promote learning in those who follow them; (b) these rules prescribe an ordered and relatively extensive set of activities to be engaged in with the intention of learning something; (c) the rules only partially specify the activities to be pursued in that they indicate the content to be studied in the learning activities. They do not necessarily indicate how the content is to be studied or what materials are to be used" (Daniels & Coombs, 1982, 255).

"Curriculum is what is successfully conveyed to differing degrees to different students, by committed teachers using appropriate materials and actions, of legitimated bodies of knowledge, skill, taste, and propensity to act and react, which are chosen for instruction after serious reflection and communal decision by representatives of those involved in the teaching of a specified group of students who are known to the decision makers" (Schwab, 1983, 240).

"The curriculum of a school, or a course, or a classroom can be conceived of as a series of planned events that are intended to have educational consequences for one or more students" (Eisner, 2002, 31).

> "A curriculum is a particular way of ordering content and purposes for teaching and learning in schools" (Walker, 2003, 4).
>
> "[Curriculum is] that reconstruction of knowledge and experience that enables the learner to grow in exercising intelligent control of subsequent knowledge and experience" (Tanner & Tanner, 2007, 99).

The existence of such a variety of definitions of curriculum makes one wonder if they all actually refer to the same phenomenon. Scholars who have studied this problem (Stenhouse, 1975; Derr, 1977; Portellli, 1987; Jackson, 1992; Walker, 2003) have concluded that the term *curriculum* is used in a multiplicity of ways, depending on the purpose of the user, and that it is futile to think that curriculum is something that needs to be defined in just one way. They believe the best that can be expected is that users of the term will define it in the specific way they intend to use it in the context in which they are working. This will be the intention in this book on a grammar of curriculum practice; our goal will be to stipulate a definition of curriculum appropriate to this particular context.[1]

Such a definition of curriculum must, first of all, be a generic definition—one that refers to the inherent nature of what might be called curriculum regardless of the features of any particular embodiment of curriculum. Whatever form, content, or purposes a particular instance of curriculum may exhibit, another instance of it can certainly exhibit a different set of features, yet both can be understood to be curriculum in a generic sense. A generic definition needs to be formulated in such a way that it can encompass every instance of the phenomenon of curriculum, regardless of their substantive differences. This calls for the identification of the essential structural elements common to all curricula.

The definitions of curriculum quoted in box 2.1 are intended to be generic ones, but given the wide range of concepts used in them, it is difficult to imagine what the common structural elements of curriculum are that these definitions are attempting to explicate. The task in providing a generic definition of curriculum is to identify its basic elements and root concepts that will give precise meaning to the term, and at the same time show how they are inherent in all instances of the phenomenon. What we seek is a set of structural concepts, as few in number as essential but as many as are necessary, so that the phenomenon of curriculum becomes fully intelligible and distinguishable from other phenomena. This task will be pursued in the remainder of this chapter, but first some additional kinds of distinctions need to be acknowledged before moving forward with stipulating a more viable generic definition of curriculum.

A satisfactory definition of something should not only clearly state what its essential internal nature is, but as has been mentioned, it should also permit one to clearly distinguish that phenomenon from other phenomena with which it might be confused (Hospers, 1967; Gorovitz, 1979). In the case of curriculum, there are a number of other terms that can refer to something similar to what curriculum might refer to, and so a definition of curriculum must establish clear boundaries between what the term shall refer to and what these other terms might refer to. A list of such terms might include, for example, *education, schooling, training, instruction, teaching, and learning*. Is the phenomenon curriculum like what any of these terms refers to? Does it overlap with any of these? Is it included within any of these? Is curriculum distinguishable from these other entities? If so, in what ways does it differ from any of these?

A good bit of analytic work has been done to try to distinguish among the usages of these terms, including the term *curriculum*. I will not attempt to retrace this work here; I will only point to some of this scholarship (see box 2.2) and indicate that much of it does help to clarify how these terms may differ regarding their referents, where there are confusing overlaps, when it may be more exact to choose one in preference over another, and why it is truly necessary to stipulate a definition of the way the user construes the meaning of the term chosen if confusion is to be avoided.

Learning, for instance, is understood to refer to the activity that occurs within an individual during times of external or internal stimulation with the intention to acquire new thoughts, information, dispositions, skills, ways of being, and so forth. Learning is a phenomenon least likely to be confused with curriculum, since it occurs much later in time than when curriculum, however defined, is planned. *Teaching and instruction* refer to actions that take place outside of instances of learning, but which are intended to assist the learner to learn. What constitutes teaching or instruction in particular instances is

---

Box 2.2
Analytic Work Done to Distinguish Sometimes Overlapping Concepts Related to Curriculum

Soltis (1978) has analyzed several educational concepts, including education, teaching, subject matter, and learning. Macmillan and Nelson (1968) included noteworthy analyses of the concept of teaching by Smith, Scheffler, Green, and Komisar, and its relation to learning and education. Biesta and Stengel (2016) noted ways teaching has been analyzed. Christiansen and Fisher (1979) and Steiner (1981) in their work on educology have partitioned several aspects of education, including differentiating curriculum from teaching and learning. Smith (1963) has focused on instruction. Gagne et al. (2005) analyze learning in relation to instruction. Johnson (1977) distinguishes curriculum from instruction. Egan (1978) notes how unhelpful it is to consider curriculum coterminous with education. Surbhi (2015) analyzes the difference between training and education. Knapp and Hopmann (2017) distinguish curriculum and Didaktik.

open to a variety of definitions, because they are not predictable processes in the sense of being guided by precise rules or conventions (instruction having this connotation more often than teaching, however). These processes involve taking into account a variety of factors both contextual and internal to the student and making considered judgments about what is best to do in providing the assistance the learner needs in order to learn. These are practices, performed by individuals or through mediated aliases, similar in kind to those practices cited earlier in this book, with their own constituent elements and grammars. *Instruction* more often than *teaching* is a term associated with skill learning, though in common practice it is often used to refer to the same activities as teaching. *Training* is the term, however, that is usually applied to the learning of skills or of a vocation rather than to learning of all kinds. It is broader in scope than teaching or instruction and is often used interchangeably (and confusingly) with the term *education*. *Education* is the most general of the terms involved in this analysis, and has been given the widest range of meanings in its usage. It can refer to any or all of the phenomena cited here (learning, teaching, instruction, training, even curriculum plans and programs). It can refer to practices and ideas involved in arranging for and conducting any of these activities, as well as to the institutions that provide these arrangements and activities. It is often a concept used to distinguish this realm of human affairs from that of other realms, such as military, legal, economic, cultural, religious, or family affairs.

So, how must a definition of curriculum be construed so that it is understood to refer to something clearly distinguishable from these other terms? A preliminary scrutiny of the definitions of curriculum quoted above would suggest that some of them incorporate facets of some of these other concepts and, therefore, do not adequately partition curriculum off from other related phenomena. A more careful analysis of these definitions will be useful in coming to a conceptualization of curriculum that is distinctive and more precise in differentiating it from other phenomena.

Table 2.1 lists four ways of conceptualizing the domain of curriculum that are derived from examining the definitions of curriculum quoted above. Other ways are quite possible as well, but these four will suffice for purposes of this analysis. The authors of the definitions of curriculum quoted above are listed in the left column. Each definition has been analyzed to determine what conceptions of the domain of curriculum appear to be reflected within that definition. The conclusions are identified by check marks placed under one or more of the four ways. Notice in table 2.1 that the domain of curriculum is inclusive of all four ways in one case (Schwab), of one way in two instances (Daniels & Coombs and Walker), of two ways in several instances, and of three ways in only two definitions (Huebner and Tanner & Tanner).

Which conception of the domain of curriculum best partitions off curriculum from other related phenomena and should be chosen as the territory about which a definition of curriculum as a distinctive phenomenon should be devised? I judge that it is the one titled Curriculum as Prescribed Plan of Action in table 2.1, not just because it has the most check marks in this analysis, but because I think it best serves the purpose of supporting the notion of curriculum practice to which this book is chiefly addressed. If a definition of curriculum were to adopt boundaries as broad as to include actual educative transactions that involve students, for example, or if teaching or instructional activities or devising curriculum proposals for possible adoption were also to be included, it would require curriculum practitioners to engage in a multiplicity of practices not solely related to the central concerns of curriculum practice. There are other designated people who regularly engage in work related to these other domains, but creating prescribed plans of action for curriculum is not the focus of their work. If this work is to be done, it requires specialists who can deal exclusively with it. The notion of curriculum practice, consequently, implies that this is a kind of practice that is not the prerogative of those who engage in teaching, instruction, being educated, or

Table 2.1. Conceptualizations of the Domain of Curriculum

Definitions	Curriculum as Proposal	Curriculum as Prescribed Plan of Action	Curriculum as Teaching/Instructional Activities	Curriculum as Educative Transaction
Faix, 1964		✓	✓	
Huebner, 1966		✓	✓	✓
Broudy, 1966		✓	✓	
Duncan & Fymier, 1967		✓		✓
Stenhouse, 1975	✓	✓		
Derr, 1977		✓		✓
Daniels & Coombs, 1982		✓		
Schwab, 1983	✓	✓	✓	✓
Eisner, 2002		✓	✓	
Walker, 2003		✓		
Tanner & Tanner, 2007		✓	✓	✓

proposing curriculum, but is one that deals exclusively with the domain of curriculum conceived of as a Prescribed Plan of Action. A definition of curriculum must, in this view, assume this conception of the domain of curriculum and will need to be commensurate with this conception.

It is also useful to acknowledge at this point in this exercise that an adequate definition of curriculum cannot be established simply by having a clear conception of the domain to which it refers. This is a necessary but insufficient condition for achieving this goal. We must also know what makes up this phenomenon. Of what sorts of things is it constituted? What are its components, and how are they structured? Are there essential elements, the absence of any one of which would prevent us from recognizing the phenomenon as a curriculum? Has the necessary empirical work been done to identify these constituent elements? Are there conflicting versions of what makes up a curriculum? If so, how are we to resolve this dilemma and arrive at a generic definition of curriculum?

It is quite rare to find empirical studies of the common elements included in more than one or two examples of actual curricula. People who have broad experience with diverse examples of curricula have been the source of most of the evidence of what makes up curricula in the generic sense. Their conceptualizations, insofar as they have attempted to explicate them, vary considerably. Curriculum scholars have been prone to conceptualize the components of curriculum on the basis of their familiarity with the phenomenon rather than from an analysis of empirical studies. This is not necessarily a bad thing, but it has resulted in lists of components of two kinds: those intended to reflect "what is" the case and those intended to suggest "what ought to be" the case. The resulting variety of conceptualizations of the essential constitutive elements of curriculum has provided curriculum practitioners with confusing options on which to base their work of preparing curricular plans.[2] Which conception is to be adopted? Why are different things named as basic components of curriculum?

Why do some have, for instance, three components that need to be included in a curriculum and others have five or ten? Is it wise to draft plans with components recommended by scholars whose list represents "what is" or by those who evidently find a "what is" list in need of revision and who recommend a "what ought to be" list? How are they to determine the conceptualization they will employ in actually constructing curriculum?

To begin to try to deal constructively with these issues, it is worthwhile to examine some of the existing conceptualizations of essential components of curriculum in some detail. Table 2.2 lists some of these in the left-hand column, identified by author and source. In the second column, I have identified the component elements of curriculum (construed generically) named by each of these authors. This brief extraction from their writings does not provide a complete picture of their conceptualizations (for this, see the sources listed), but this listing should suffice for the purpose of analyzing the primary commonalities and differences among them.

Table 2.3 lists twelve categories of elements found in the conceptualizations of what curriculum consists of, as stated by the authors listed in table 2.2. Listed for each category are the authors who identify some component of curriculum that falls within that category. In doing an initial analysis of this information, it is perhaps surprising to find that only "content or subject matter" is identified by all of these authors. This component of curriculum is so widely acknowledged that it is often assumed by laypersons (and by some professionals) that the only thing that needs to be specified in producing a curriculum is the content or subject matter component. These curriculum scholars identify several other things, however, that they think should be included, though differing considerably in which ones and how many to include. Further analysis of these categories of named components should lead to some conclusions about which ones and how many are inherently essential in defining what constitutes a curriculum.

Because matters of learning, teaching, and instruction were determined to lie outside the domain of curriculum in the ear-

Table 2.2. Curriculum Components

Herrick, 1950	a learner, a purpose, a content, a process
Duncan & Frymier, 1967	actors, artifacts, operations
Zais, 1976	goals, objectives, content, learning activities, evaluation
Johnson, 1977	intended learning outcomes, selected cultural content, structural organization, evaluation
Goodlad, 1979	goals/objectives/purposes, content, materials, learning activities, teaching strategies, evaluation, grouping, time, space, contextual influences
Beauchamp, 1981	cultural content, goals and/or objectives, purposes, evaluation scheme
Frymier, 1986	purposes, substance, methods of teaching, objectives, materials
Schubert, 1986	purpose, content or learning experiences, organization, evaluation
Doyle, 1986	a product, operations to produce a product, resources, their significance
Macdonald, 1986	situations (dynamic interaction of events and actions), events (patterns of actions), actions (transactions within events), all constructed as ethical actions
Foshay, 1987	purposes, substance, practices (each having subelements)
Eash, 1991	assumptions about learner and society, aims and objectives, content (selection, scope, sequence), modes of transaction by teacher, evaluation
Huebner, 1999	educative content, made present through consciously constructed environments, for particular educatees, within particular arrangements for governing power between educator and educatees

van den Akker, 2003	rationale, aims and objectives, content, learning activities, teacher role, materials and resources, grouping, location, time, assessment
Posner, 2004	objectives, rationale or philosophy, content, characteristics of target audience, activities, materials, sequencing principles, schedule, teacher training, evaluation, administrative matters, relation of the parts

Table 2.3. Authors Identifying Curriculum Components by Category

Learning activities engaged in by students	All except Johnson, 1977; Beauchamp, 1981; Frymier, 1986; Doyle, 1986; Eash, 1991
Learning outcomes or objectives for students	Zais, 1976; Johnson, 1977; Goodlad, 1979; Beauchamp, 1981; Frymier, 1986; Doyle, 1986; van den Akker, 2003; Posner, 2004
Teaching activities, plans, methods, materials	Herrick, 1950; Duncan & Frymier, 1967; Goodlad, 1979; Frymier, 1986; Doyle, 1986; Macdonald, 1986; Foshay, 1987; Eash, 1991; Huebner, 1999; van den Akker, 2003; Posner, 2004
Content or subject matter	All except Macdonald, 1986 (included, however, in Macdonald, 1967)
Organization of content or subject matter	Duncan & Frymier, 1967; Johnson, 1977; Goodlad, 1979; Schubert, 1986; Doyle, 1986; Macdonald, 1986; Foshay, 1987; Eash, 1991; Poser, 2004
Assumptions about learners, society, knowledge, values, etc.	Johnson, 1977; Macdonald, 1986; Eash, 1991

continued on next page

Table 2.3. Continued

Contextual influences or considerations	Goodlad, 1979; Macdonald, 1986
Evaluation	Zais, 1976; Johnson, 1977; Goodlad, 1979; Beauchamp, 1981; Schubert, 1986; Foshay, 1987; Eash, 1991; van den Akker, 2003; Posner, 2004
Administrative arrangements	Duncan & Frymier, 1967; Goodlad, 1979; Foshay, 1987; Huebner, 1999; van den Akker, 2003; Posner, 2004
Purposes or long-range goals	Herrick, 1950; Zais, 1976; Goodlad, 1979; Beauchamp, 1981; Frymier, 1986; Schubert, 1986; Macdonald, 1986; Foshay, 1987; Eash, 1991; van den Akker, 2003; Posner, 2004
Rationale	Doyle, 1986; van den Akker, 2003; Posner, 2004
Interrelationship among components	Posner, 2004

lier analysis of that topic, in this analysis of the components of curriculum the first three components listed in table 2.3 must be excluded as not being within the scope of what internally constitutes a curriculum (that is, learning activities, learning outcomes, and teaching activities are not to be considered components of curriculum).[3] So what about the rest of the components in the list? Let us consider them one by one.

Constituent Components of a Curriculum

Most recognized and most often listed as a component of curriculum is *curriculum content* or *subject matter*. Such is the case, one may presume, because students must interact with something if they are to learn anything. Precisely what this substantive component needs to be, however, is a matter to be determined at the point of contact in the immediate educative environment in which the content, the teacher, or other media or stimuli are made present for the student to interact with. This substantive dimension, if it is to be included at all as a component of curriculum as a Prescribed Plan of Action in advance of the actual educative situation, must be defined at a more general level of conceptualization, the specific formulation of which should be capable of giving guidance on the overall parameters of the content to be chosen, specifying the way this substantive component is to be conceived and used, and providing adequate justifications for how it is conceptualized. I do think this is an essential component of curriculum, if defined as follows.

THE SUBSTANTIVE COMPONENT

The substantive component of curriculum is stipulated to be the prescribed nature, form, kind, extent, use, and rationale of the subject matter content (conceptualized in general terms) that is to be made available in the educative settings in which the curriculum is to be enacted.

This component provides direction and guidance for the choices and allocation of specific subject matter content for particular levels or arrangements of schooling or educational situations as they may be configured in the actual enactment of the curriculum. It addresses the several generic features mentioned but does not get into prescribing particular subject matter content for teaching, instruction, or learning. In addition, this definition is intended to be construed broadly enough that any and all notions of subject matter content, however they may differ philosophically or pragmatically, can be acknowledged within the definition and can be stated in whatever terms their prescribers wish to do so. The definition is meant to be conceptually neutral. (This will also be the intention with all the definitions of the components of curriculum that are given in this chapter.)

The second most mentioned component in table 2.3 is *purposes* or *long-range goals*. Inevitably, a curriculum is designed to accomplish some purpose(s) or long-range goal(s). Just what those purposes or long-range goals should be needs to be prescribed in clear and unambiguous terms as an essential component of a curriculum. The literature regarding this topic uses terms such as *goals, aims, objectives*, as well as the more general term *purposes*. Sometimes they appear to be used interchangeably, and sometimes they refer to somewhat different levels or kinds of expectations. These terms have also been used in connection with teaching, learning, and instruction, where their meaning is clearly not the same as when used in connection with curriculum. Can the distinctions be sorted out? How should this component of curriculum be conceptualized so that the terms used are clearly defined and do not signal the same things as do the terms used during enactment of a curriculum?

An analysis of the role this component of curriculum plays in the overall conceptualization a curriculum suggests that it is to be prescribed for the purpose of setting the general direction the entire curriculum is to take, while at the same time limiting the interpretation of these prescriptions so that they will focus on the exact meaning intended and not be interpreted more narrowly or more broadly than they are meant to be. These prescriptions are not meant to state particular outcomes (even long-range ones) that the curriculum is expected to achieve. Rather, they give definition to the vision of the entire curriculum and its purpose. They provide essential conceptions of what will make a particular curriculum unique, and not to be confused with some other version of a curriculum. They provide the underlying focus and rationale for the scope of the various long-range prescriptions made for the entire curriculum. They provide a means by which those who plan all parts of a curriculum can keep an eye on what was the original intent of those who envisioned the curriculum. Similarly, those who enact the curriculum can return to the conceptualization of this component to check on whether their work is consistent with the prescribed intent. I choose to define this component of curriculum as follows.

THE INTENTIONAL COMPONENT

The intentional component of curriculum is stipulated to be the prescribed purpose, unique objective(s), and accompanying rationale intended to govern all aspects of planning and enactment of the curriculum.

Looking at another possible component of curriculum, it is often considered to be optional whether identifying the various assumptions that underlie the prescriptions set forth in a curriculum should be included as essential. The best argument for including this would appear to be that doing so allows anyone to better understand why the various things in the curriculum are to be enacted as prescribed. In the absence of such information, it is quite possible that planners or enactors of the curriculum will incorrectly infer what is consistent with the prescriptions because there are no explicit statements to the contrary. Stated in positive terms, inferences about what is consistent with the prescriptions set forth in a curriculum can be checked by reference to relevant assumptions that have been deliberately included. By including key assumptions on which the curriculum is based, the intentional component of curriculum is effectively reinforced; the reasoning behind what keeps all curricular choices consistent with the stated purpose becomes clearer when the assumptions on which they are based are available for examination, and speculation about what they are does not have to occur.

If we ask what the topics are about which assumptions should be stated and included in a curriculum, it is undoubtedly wise to say that no definitive list should be expected to be identified as required. Among the more common ones are assumptions about learners, about knowledge, about teaching, about schooling, about democracy, about values such as equity, equality, freedom, and so on. What kinds of assumptions and what particular assumptions are to be included as a component of curriculum are surely to be determined by the inherent requirements of the prescriptions being presented in the various aspects of the curriculum. The rule might be: whatever will help make clear the basis for these various prescriptions. In light of these analytic observations, I choose to define this component of curriculum as follows.

THE ASSUMPTIVE COMPONENT

The assumptive component of curriculum is stipulated to be the selected set of assumptions required to make clear the reasoning behind the various choices made throughout the curriculum, based on what is taken to be true in relevant domains of reference.

Another possible component of curriculum identified in table 2.3 is concerned with matters that exist in the external world that can affect what is prescribed in a curriculum. These contextual realities or influences can be of several kinds depending on whether one is considering the immediate local setting, a broader social/regional/national context, or a more global frame of reference. In contrast to the kinds of things identified in the assumptive component of curriculum (where alternatives exist and a choice among them has to be made explicit), in the case of contextual realities and influences, we are referring to factual matters where empirical scholarship can in most cases identify precisely what the reality is in a given circumstance and where the results are not matters of subjective preference or interpretation. What types of contextual facts might appropriately be referred to? What particular facts in any of these categories should be identified when addressing this component of curriculum? Why include them at all?

Some factual realms that might conceivably be pertinent to how a curriculum is constructed include the following: student demographic trends, postgraduation educational and employment opportunities, community/societal expectations, cultural norms/practices of relevant student groupings, other educational opportunities in the community; prevailing views of national authority (e.g., democratic, dictatorial), global/national/local crises being faced, nature and stability of financial support for curriculum, quality and capability of teaching (and other associated) personnel, social/economic status of those for whom the curriculum is intended, and more. By precisely acknowledging and explicitly stating the factual realities that exist in a given curricular context, it should be possible to see how the particular prescriptions made throughout a curriculum are consistent with the actual realities and not leave one wondering what factual realities were implicitly assumed. If any curriculum were to avoid including this component, it could easily be challenged as being too idealistic or too removed from the realities in which it is situated for it to be successfully enacted and its stated intentions fully realized. A generic conceptualization of this component can neither specify what particular set of contextual factors needs to be addressed, nor how many specific factual statements need to be included when planning each and every curriculum. These determinations must be made in the process of planning a particular curriculum, and they will depend on discerning what will give credibility to the prescriptions made (and to the arguments made for them) in the various other components of the curriculum. I think this component of curriculum should be included and should be defined as follows.

THE CONTEXTUAL REALITIES COMPONENT

The contextual realities component of curriculum is stipulated to be the selected set of factual statements required to make clear the factors external to the curriculum (the empirical realities) that are taken into account in making the prescriptions throughout the curriculum.

The way a curriculum is to be organized is usually considered to be one of its essential components. This component has to do primarily with prescribing how the subject matter content (the substantive component) is to be organized across time and circumstances. Because a curriculum is planned to extend over a great many years, because it necessarily must be broken into a number of shorter-term blocks of time, and because these blocks of time must accommodate a variety of learning situations (as may be required by differing student progress over time), some particular way of organizing the subject matter content and related matters must be identified and prescribed.

A given set of prescribed subject matter content can conceivably be arranged to be encountered by students in a great many different ways. What is the preferred way of organizing the substantive component as conceived by the planners? Is there anything stated in the prescriptions for the intentional, assumptive, or substantive components of the curriculum that would seem to require a specific way of organizing the curriculum if those prescriptions are to be enacted appropriately? If so, what organizational arrangement should be explicitly prescribed in the organizational component? If not, what sort of organizational flexibility is explicitly permitted?

This component is concerned with organizing curricular content in the broadest of terms—for the entire span of the curriculum and not just for particular levels or particular subjects, or particular years or particular student groupings. These particular matters are to be addressed when arranging for enactment of a curriculum. Some traditional models for organizing curriculum content have been labeled "subject organization," "discipline-centered organization," "broad fields organization," "core curriculum," "integrated curriculum," and "spiral curriculum." These models are by no means the only possibilities that exist or could be conceived. Whatever organizational scheme is prescribed for a particular curriculum, it must be consistent with and facilitate the unique purpose of the curriculum. It must also be consonant with what is prescribed in the subject matter content component and contribute to its clarity rather than cause confusion by appearing to be better suited to some other conception of the content.

The prescriptions for how curriculum is to be organized must also specify how students are to move through the subject matter content as it is conceived and structured. For instance, what is reserved for early education, middle education, or later education if distinctive levels or blocks of education such as these are prescribed? Is there to be a portion of the curriculum devoted to general education, to specialized education, to exploratory education, or to student-chosen enrichment education? If so, where does each occur and for what span of time? Are there multiple routes through these levels or types of education that will allow different groups of students or individual students to encounter the subject matter in different ways or at different times, as may be required for reasons of student developmental maturity, preference, or organizational efficiency? A full articulation of how this organizational component of curriculum is to be conceived and prescribed is required (not necessarily relying on conventional terminology, using new labels if needed). And some persuasive rationale for the prescribed organizational scheme also needs to be included. I affirm that this component of curriculum should be included and defined as follows.

THE ORGANIZATIONAL COMPONENT

The organizational component of curriculum is stipulated to be the prescribed way of structuring the entire curriculum so that its subject matter content is explicitly organized for matriculation by students as they work over time to achieve the stated purpose and unique objectives of the curriculum.

Despite the fact that it was stipulated earlier in this book that the domain of curriculum should exclude educational practices related to the educative transactions of the learner as well as those of the educators who directly interact with the learner, it is possible that the action plans prescribed in a curriculum might include some guidelines for its enactment related to teaching and learning. Consequently, we should consider whether these two topics should be stipulated as essential components of curriculum as well.

Are there, for instance, particular ways in which the student's educational situation, activities, or processes should be conceived if the vision of curriculum explicated in its various other components is to be authentically enacted? Are there unique requirements for how learning environments are to be designed that derive from the curriculum's purpose, unique objectives, notions of content, or overall structure? Should certain practices in that domain be deliberately prohibited? Certain prescriptions about what is or is not to occur in the transactions the student will engage in will be of assistance in keeping practices in this domain consistent with the curriculum as planned. They can take the form of general statements or perhaps even quite particular prescriptions if deemed necessary.

Similarly, with respect to teaching practices, are there particular approaches, methods, materials, media, or other forms of educative procedures that the curriculum as envisioned would uniquely require if it is to be enacted authentically? Is any such activity to be proscribed? Again, it would seem to be most helpful from the point of view of practitioners engaged in teaching to have explicit guidelines for what is uniquely necessary in their domain if their practices are to be consistent with the curriculum as conceptualized—while leaving all other decisions involved up to their own discretion. Therefore, I choose to include these two matters as essential components of curriculum and wish to define them as follows.

The Student Transactive Component

The student transactive component of curriculum is stipulated to be the prescribed ways the student learning situation, activities, or processes are to be conceived and designed (if any) so that they uniquely facilitate the authentic enactment of the curriculum.

The Teaching Transactive Component

The teaching transactive component of curriculum is stipulated to be the prescribed ways the teaching methods, materials, media, or other procedures employed as stimuli in the student transactive component are to be conceived and designed (if any) so that they uniquely facilitate the authentic enactment of the curriculum.

Another component of curriculum identified in table 2.3 by several authors is that of curriculum evaluation. It is true that a great many action plans for curriculum are put together without including this component. Nevertheless, if it is ever to be determined whether a curriculum is enacted in keeping with its stated purpose, unique objectives, content, structure, assumptions, contextual realities, and so on, some plan for assessing these matters seems to be required. Some explicit prescriptions for doing this kind of evaluation are essential for making subsequent changes or improvements in the Prescribed Action Plan for a curriculum. What data-gathering procedures are to be conducted and on what topics? Have the intended purpose, unique objectives, assumptions, values, and so forth been adhered to? When, under what circumstances, and by whom should these data be gathered? Should student achievement data be considered? Who is to analyze the data and draw conclusions about whether enactment has been done appropriately? Or if it has not been done appropriately, is it due to the practices of teachers, students, or others, or a result of there being unclear or erroneous prescriptions contained in the curriculum plan itself? When does evaluation data suggest that more than a minor revision of the Prescribed Action Plan is required, perhaps a full replacement with another entirely different one based on quite different conceptions of what should be prescribed in the various components of curriculum? All this work should not be left to specialists outside the domain of curriculum; it should be conducted by curriculum practitioners themselves, who have the mandate and the experience to create, evaluate, revise, or plan a new curriculum. In my judgment, curriculum evaluation is an essential component of curriculum, and I choose to define it as follows.

THE EVALUATION COMPONENT

The evaluation component of curriculum is stipulated to be the prescribed methods of collecting, analyzing, and making evaluative judgments on data intended to determine whether a curriculum has been enacted as conceived and planned or whether it needs to be revised in part or in its entirety.

Administrative arrangements for enacting a curriculum are considered to be a component of curriculum by some but not all authors listed in table 2.3. Clearly, carrying out supportive administrative arrangements related to curriculum planning and enactment falls outside the domain of curriculum practice per se, and is usually considered to be the province of administrative personnel with knowledge and skills in that domain. However, if there are special administrative arrangements that a curriculum plan wishes to prescribe as uniquely necessary for it to be enacted appropriately, then such prescriptions should be stated and justified. This will alert administrators to special actions that must be taken above and beyond what is normally required to support the work of any educational organization. I am persuaded that this topic deserves to be addressed in an essential component of curriculum and choose to define it as follows.

THE SUPPORTIVE ARRANGEMENTS COMPONENT

The supportive arrangements component of curriculum is stipulated to be the prescribed set of time, facilities, personnel, teaching/learning resources, financial, organizational, and legitimating arrangements that is uniquely required (if any) to support the development and enactment of the curriculum.

The decision of whether to identify "rationale" as a separate component of curriculum or to consider it part of what is addressed in each and every other component of curriculum is perhaps a matter of personal preference. Without question, however, inclusion of robust statements justifying the assertions and prescriptions made throughout a curriculum is essential if they are to be clearly understood, agreed to, and appropriately acted on. If the matters specified in various components of a curriculum are not persuasively argued for or are not argued for at all, chances are good that the prescriptions will not be accepted or adhered to faithfully in attempts to enact them. It may be not be hyperbole to say that without statements justifying everything prescribed in a curriculum, curriculum enactors are likely to deviate radically from what was intended by the planners and not even realize they are doing so. By having such statements conveniently at hand, they will be less likely to ignore them or misinterpret them. And they will be more likely to see how the various components hang together if an overall statement of rationale is included. I believe there should be a component of curriculum that offers a coherent rationale for the entire curriculum, including justification for every prescription it sets forth. I choose to define this component of curriculum as follows.

THE JUSTIFICATION COMPONENT

The justification component of curriculum is stipulated to be the array of reasons given for each and every assertion and prescription made in each and every component of the curriculum that will provide persuasive and coherent arguments for accepting and enacting the entire curriculum as prescribed.

I come now in this effort to conceptualize what constitutes a curriculum to the task of explaining why I accept the previous list of ten components of curriculum as those that are essential to defining its nature and structure. Some of the listed components can more readily be accepted than others by virtue of their prima facie identification with ordinary uses of the term *curriculum*—for instance, the substantive, the intentional, and the organizational components. Without these, a curriculum surely does not exist. I would argue that the justification component is also a crucial component of what constitutes a complete conceptualization of curriculum for the reason that its clarity and motive for acceptance and enactment largely depend on how well the various prescriptions it includes are explained and argued for. Failure to be accepted or enacted appropriately can usually be traced to a lack of sufficient or compelling arguments having been explicitly stated. The assumptive component and the contextual realities component are essential for similar reasons. If matters related to these two components are left unstated or are unclearly stated, the prescribed actions set forth in other parts of a curriculum may not be understood correctly, may seem arbitrary, or may even be ignored as insignificant due to the fact that an explicit basis and supportive reasoning are lacking. When it comes to deciding whether the remaining four components (the student transactive component, the teaching transactive component, the evaluation component, and the supportive arrangements component) are indeed essential elements of a curriculum, I would argue that they are essential on the basis of pragmatic considerations. All too often curriculum plans are conceived without explicitly dealing with these matters, and the result is that those who have the responsibility for enacting and supporting the planned curriculum are left to imagine what might be appropriate in these realms; they can often misconstrue what is consistent with its intended prescriptions, and thus, inadvertently, undermine its effective enactment. Conversely, it can be said that if a curriculum plan addresses these components with explicit prescriptions, the plan is more likely to be enacted and supported appropriately and effectively. Curriculum designers need to have a realistic understanding of what those who will utilize it and enact it have to deal with in practical terms such that sufficient practical guidance is offered to them and they will think the plan is realistic and actionable. Inclusion of these four components should supply evidence to this effect.

Table 2.4 recaps the ten essential components of curriculum as I have stipulated them and orders them in a way that might suggest that they should be addressed in this prescribed sequence. However, no such prescribed sequence is intended. It is quite possible that when a curriculum (A Prescribed Action Plan) is put together, work can be done on any or several of the components without reference to which comes first, second, and so on. The key is that in the end all parts are consistent and interrelated with one another. (Note that I have not identified "the interrelationship among components" listed in table 2.3 as

How Curriculum Is to Be Defined | 41

Table 2.4. Ten Essential Components of Curriculum

1. The Intentional Component: *The intentional component of curriculum is stipulated to be the prescribed purpose, unique objective(s), and accompanying rationale intended to govern all aspects of planning and enactment of the curriculum.*

2. The Organizational Component: *The organizational component of curriculum is stipulated to be the prescribed way of structuring the entire curriculum so that its subject matter content is explicitly organized for matriculation by students as they work over time to achieve the stated purpose and unique objectives of the curriculum.*

3. The Substantive Component: *The substantive component of curriculum is stipulated to be the prescribed nature, form, kind, extent, use, and rationale of the subject matter content (conceptualized in general terms) that is to be made available in the educative settings in which the curriculum is to be enacted.*

4. The Assumptive Component: *The assumptive component of curriculum is stipulated to be the selected set of assumptions required to make clear the reasoning behind the various choices made throughout the curriculum, based on what is taken to be true in relevant domains of reference.*

5. The Contextual Realities Component: *The contextual realities component of curriculum is stipulated to be the selected set of factual statements required to make clear the factors external to the curriculum (the empirical realities) that are taken into account in making the prescriptions throughout the curriculum.*

6. The Student Transactive Component: *The student transactive component of curriculum is stipulated to be the prescribed ways the student learning situation, activities, or processes are to be conceived and designed (if any) so that they uniquely facilitate the authentic enactment of the curriculum.*

7. The Teaching Transactive Component: *The teaching transactive component of curriculum is stipulated to be the prescribed ways the teaching methods, materials, media, or other procedures employed as stimuli in the student transactive component are to be conceived and designed (if any) so that they uniquely facilitate the authentic enactment of the curriculum.*

continued on next page

Table 2.4. Continued

8. The Evaluation Component: *The evaluation component of curriculum is stipulated to be the prescribed methods of collecting, analyzing, and making evaluative judgments on data intended to determine whether a curriculum has been enacted as conceived and planned or whether it needs to be revised in part or in its entirety.*
9. The Supportive Arrangements Component: *The supportive arrangements component of curriculum is stipulated to be the prescribed set of time, facilities, personnel, teaching/learning resources, financial, organizational, and legitimating arrangements that is uniquely required (if any) to support the development and enactment of the curriculum.*
10. The Justification Component: *The justification component of curriculum is stipulated to be the array of reasons given for each and every assertion and prescription made in each and every component of the curriculum that will provide persuasive and coherent arguments for accepting and enacting the entire curriculum as prescribed.*

an essential component of curriculum, not because this is not of great significance, but because it just does not seem to qualify as a component about which something can be prescribed. It is more like a characteristic of curriculum that is attended to in the course of putting together the whole curriculum plan.)

The only reason for listing the components in table 2.4 in the order in which they appear is that the choices made for each successive component depend to a certain extent on the choices made in the previous components (and on their justification); thus the logic of these choices is made clearer. So, prescriptions about the organizational structure of curriculum must be consistent with prescriptions on its focal purpose and objectives. Prescriptions about the substance of curriculum must be consistent with the preceding two components (intentional and organizational). Assumptions must be consistent with the intentional, the organizational, and the substantive components. Facts identified in the contextual realities component must deal with matters arising in connection with the previous four components. And, in like manner, the prescriptions made in the remaining components listed need to be consistent with all of the components that precede each of them. The exception to this line of argument may be component ten: the justification component. While the justifications presented for the assertions and prescriptions made in each component of curriculum need to be consistent with those made in every other component, the arguments made in each case must stand on their own and do not follow logically from those in preceding components. However, whatever rationale is given for the whole of the curriculum must certainly depend on and be consistent with all of the justifications offered in the preceding components. To make clear the unique role of component ten in the overall definition of curriculum as conceptualized in this book, the visual portrayal presented in figure 2.1 will be helpful. Its place at the center

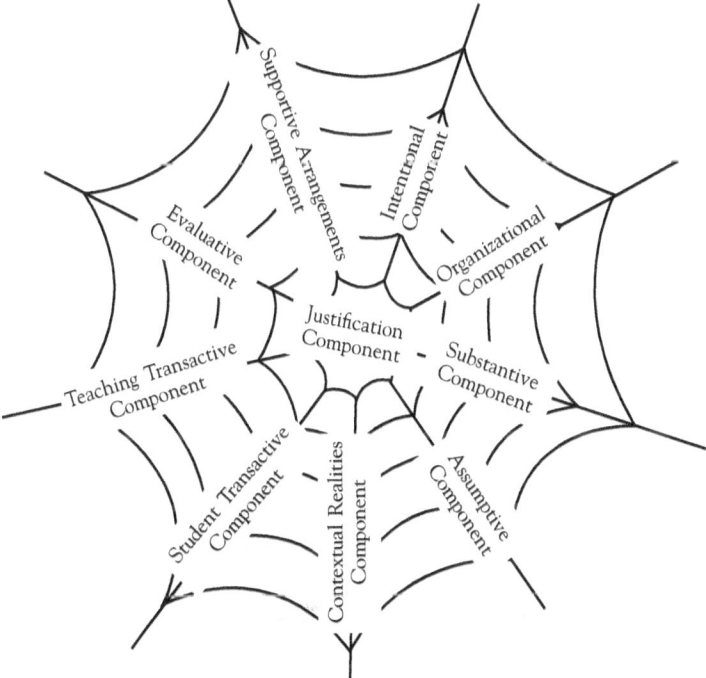

Figure 2.1. Web of curriculum components. Based on design by van den Akker (2003, p. 6).

emphasizes the fact that the justification is part of every component and of the whole curriculum as well. The idea that there are interrelationships among all the components is conveyed by their depiction as parts of an interconnected web.

How, then, is curriculum to be defined? On the basis of the various analyses presented in this chapter, I am convinced that curriculum should be defined as follows:

> *Curriculum is stipulated to be a ten-category set of prescribed conceptions and actions intended to communicate in programmatic terms how a preferred conception of education is to be realized in practice— the ten categories being all the essential constitutive components required for distinguishing curriculum from other phenomena.* (See list of components and their definitions in table 2.4).

While the meaning of the concepts appearing in this definition should be evident from what has been presented earlier in this chapter, it may be helpful to parse this definition more fully in order to assure that these meanings are clearly understood.

What is meant by the phrase "ten-category set" is explained in the latter part of the definition, so that its referent is clearly identified within the definition itself and the meaning of this phrase is not left to chance. It is too cumbersome, however, to include within this definition the listing of all ten of the components of curriculum that must be addressed in planning curriculum, and so the definition necessarily points to an external listing of these components in order that "ten-category set" can be fully understood.

The phrase "prescribed conceptions and actions" refers to the type of statements that are to be produced when explicating what is envisioned for each and every component of curriculum being addressed. These statements are construed to be prescriptive in nature; that is, they are to set forth what is preferred and sanctioned as most desirable among all possible options. These statements may prescribe preferred conceptions, preferred actions, or both. They can be as numerous or as few as deemed appropriate.

The phrase "intended to communicate in programmatic terms" refers to the form the prescriptive statements should take. They should be stated at a practical or concrete level of expression rather than at a highly visionary, overly general, or vaguely discernible level. The intent of these prescriptive statements is understood to be for their application in an actual program of education, not formulated for some other purpose, such as for speculation or debate.

The phrase "how a preferred conception of education is to be realized in practice" refers to the content of the prescriptive statements that are presented in all components of curriculum. What is called for here is the prescribing of specific ideas, concepts, and actions that are to be enacted in real settings when the curriculum is being realized in practice. These prescriptions are the heart of the intended curriculum and need to be as detailed as possible, without inhibiting the use of discretion where necessary in implementing the stated prescriptions.

We have now come to the end of the chapter devoted to how curriculum is to be defined.[4] In the next chapter, the definition of practice that was earlier stipulated and the definition of curriculum stipulated in this chapter will be combined in attempting to determine the nature of curriculum practice.

Chapter 3

How Curriculum Practice Is to Be Defined

How curriculum practice is to be defined in this book is based on the definitions of practice and of curriculum that have been presented in previous chapters. For convenient reference, these two definitions are restated here.

> A *practice* is a series of sayings and doings undertaken by a person or persons to accomplish an intended purpose in a given domain of socially valued activity.

> *Curriculum* is stipulated to be a ten-category set of prescribed conceptions and actions intended to communicate in programmatic terms how a preferred conception of education is to be realized in practice—the ten categories being all the essential constitutive components required for distinguishing curriculum from other phenomena.

By simply combining these two definitions, a tentative definition of curriculum practice can be stated as follows:

> *Curriculum practice* is defined as the series of sayings and doings that is involved in prescribing the preferred conceptions and actions for all ten curriculum com-

ponents that persons conducting curriculum practice must engage in if the intended purposes of this practice are to be accomplished.

This way of defining curriculum practice is certainly more precise than the way(s) it has conventionally been understood in the informal parlance of curriculum planning, curriculum designing, curriculum development, and so on, as alluded to in the opening paragraphs of this book. Yet, does this formulation of what curriculum practice is provide as exact an account of what is to be done in curriculum practice as those who engage in it might require? What precisely is meant by the phrase "the series of sayings and doings" in the context of doing curriculum work? Are there guidelines for conducting curriculum practice that can be derived from the inherent nature of curriculum as here defined? Are there dos and don'ts for what should be said or done in curriculum practice? How can curriculum practitioners discern what prescriptions are appropriate to promulgate on a given matter related to a given component of curriculum? These and related questions suggest that further analysis of what curriculum practice entails is needed before a viable definition of curriculum practice can be stipulated.

Let us first review some of the conceptions of what is said and done in curriculum practice as presented by curriculum scholars who have studied this phenomenon or who have experienced it in a number of different locales or circumstances. Sources consulted for this purpose are separated into two categories—those where the conceptions are based on firsthand experience in doing curriculum work (the more numerous of the two) and those where they are based on formal case-study analysis of curriculum practice.

Scholars in the first category sometimes perceive curriculum work as being so complex that an entire textbook is required to explain what is involved in doing this activity (see box 3.1), while others are more succinct. In box 3.2, key concepts from an array of these conceptualizations of what constitutes curriculum work are listed for purposes of comparison and analysis.

Box 3.1
Textbooks Explaining How Curriculum Development Can Be Conceptualized

Bobbitt, 1924; Rugg, 1927; Hopkins, 1929; Smith, Stanley, & Shores, 1950; Taba, 1962; Saylor & Alexander, 1966; Macagnoni, 1970; Lewis & Miel, 1972; Reid, 1975; Oliver, 1977; Siegel, 1977; Walker, 1979; Stellar, 1983; Gay, 1984; Glatthorn, 1987; Eraut, 1990; Marsh et al., 1990; Doll, 1996; Marshall, Sears, & Schubert, 2000; Eisner, 2002; Kuiper et al., 2003; Walker, 2003; Hlebowitsh, 2005; Marsh & Willis, 2007; Tanner & Tanner, 2007; Thijs & van den Aker (2009); Glatthorn et al., 2018; and Gordon, Taylor, & Oliva, 2019.

Box 3.2
Key Concepts in Curriculum Work as Perceived by Curriculum Experts

Tyler (1949) conceived of curriculum planning as following certain procedures to obtain answers to four fundamental questions (about purposes, content, organization, and evaluation).

Herrick (1950) considered curriculum designing to be a process of making consistent decisions about the relationships among elements of the curriculum.

Taba (1962) identified a seven-step sequential process involving (1) diagnosing needs, (2) formulating objectives, (3) selecting content, (4) organizing content, (5) selecting learning experiences, (6) organizing learning activities, and (7) evaluating the resulting outcomes.

Johnson (1967) saw curriculum development as a set of procedural decision-making steps for selecting and structuring curriculum objectives and content.

Schwab (1969) asserted that curriculum planning is a practical art that requires deliberation over alternative solutions to curriculum problems based on multiple considerations and data sources.

Walker (1971, 52) claimed that curriculum development is composed of three elements: "the curriculum's platform, its design, and the deliberation associated with it." A platform consists of conceptions, theories, and aims. Like Schwab, Walker identified the concept of deliberation as key to designing and justifying curriculum.

Reid (1978) conceived of curriculum work as the solving of curriculum problems through taking action. Deliberation is required to resolve differences over which actions should be taken.

Goodlad (1979) stated that curriculum development can mean a step-by-step arranging for a sequenced program of study such as "reading," or it can mean a broad array of work to develop programs of study for an entire nation at all levels of education, or it can mean work that falls anywhere between these two; it can also mean the sociopolitical processes involved in performing these steps. Fundamentally, Goodlad identified decision-making as the central activity of curriculum work.

Walker (1979) listed four tasks: identifying need, examining and selecting a generic model, developing plans and materials that adapt the model to site-specific conditions, and implementing the plans.

Eisner (1979, 108) defined curriculum development as "the process of transforming images and aspirations about education into programs that will effectively realize the visions that initiated the process." The chief means by which this work is accomplished in Eisner's conceptualization is by the making of decisions in all the dimensions of curriculum (conceived quite like those asserted by Tyler and Taba).

Skilbeck (1982, 25–27) asserted that curriculum development consists of five stages: "situational analysis, goal formulation, program building, implementation, and evaluation."

Steller (1983, 69) stated that curriculum development involves "clarification of the current status of the prescribed educational program, deciding what that program should be, and then determining how to get there." He listed eight stages in curriculum planning: "formulation and/or review of ongoing guiding statements, assessment of progress, setting priorities, developing goals and objectives, selecting from alternatives, action planning, implementation, and monitoring/evaluating/recycling" (82).

Gay (1984, 1176) defined curriculum development as "a dynamic process of political, social, and personal negotiations that must occur in a cooperative and collaborative context if it is to produce viable educational plans."

Macdonald and Purpel (1987) believed that curriculum planning requires the articulation of a vision and a platform (a framework of assumptions and values) on the basis of which, through a process of open dialogue on issues of curriculum, shared decisions are agreed on. Elsewhere Macdonald (1986) identifies these issues as the events and actions that are ethically desirable in the actual learning environment being addressed as decided by the participants in that environment.

Eraut (1990) urged a four-step design process that includes problem formation, brainstorming, and creation of several prototypes, settling on one with the most advantages, and detailing it for implementation.

Kunzli quoted in Rosenmund (2002, 291) defined curriculum work as "the complex social process of selecting and weighing socially available knowledge and know-how aiming at concrete educational practice and expecting possible educational outcomes."

Marsh and Willis (2007, 148) defined curriculum development as "a collective and intentional process or activity directed at beneficial curriculum change."

Tanner and Tanner (2007, 444) asserted that "curriculum development may be profitably viewed as an endless problem-solving process."

Westbury (2008, 50) stated, "The idea of curriculum making captures a wide-ranging set of activities and processes emerging within webs of societal and cultural ideologies and symbols, politics and organized interest groups, organizational and administrative structures and processes, and local understandings, beliefs, and practices." He further stated that curriculum making is "a mechanism deployed to manage the political, professional, and public fields around schooling, more often than not designed to mute rather than amplify calls for educational reform and change" (61). Thus, it is a form of problem solving.

Van den Akker (2010) advocated the use of design principles such as employed in technological invention. This approach is defined as "an iterative process of 'successive approximation' or 'evolutionary prototyping' of the 'ideal' intervention" until a product that achieves the purposes sought is arrived at. A trial version of a curriculum with specific substantive and procedural characteristics and grounded with particular theoretical and empirical arguments is tested and revised continually over time. This is a strategy for ongoing curriculum revision rather than for one-time curriculum development.

Biesta (2013) defines the doing of curriculum as deliberating about the purposes and content (the ends and means) of education and not as following processes or techniques.

The second category of conceptions of what constitutes curriculum practice to be examined here pertains to discoveries arrived at through survey and case-study research and analysis. The results of these studies are listed in box 3.3 for review and further analysis.[1]

This long list of conceptions of curriculum practice presented by curriculum scholars over many decades exhibits no clear consensus among them. In fact, the diversity of conceptions is quite remarkable considering that their authors have tried to define a singular phenomenon—curriculum practice. What are

Box 3.3
Key Concepts in Curriculum Work Derived from Empirical Studies

Eible and Zavarella (1979, 86) reported that their Curriculum Review Committee "functions primarily to determine district curriculum priorities and to review proposals for curriculum change. In addition, the Committee serves to determine appropriate evaluation procedures for program changes."

Klein and Goodlad (1979, 265) studied work done in curriculum development centers in eighteen countries and found these common activities: "conducting educational needs assessments for the nation, identifying curriculum goals, reviewing and assessing current curricula, planning new curricula to be implemented in the future, defining and improving content for new curricula, developing teacher's guides and syllabuses, improving teaching methods to be used in the implementation of new curricula, and developing media and print materials to accompany curricular plans."

Wilson (1979) reported work done in a local Board of Education over several years to redesign its K–12 curriculum in ten subject areas. This work involved making decisions about content, objectives, organization, and evaluation based on district goals and values. Plans were produced through a rational transactional and interpretive process intended to translate broad policy statements into more subject-specific and classroom-specific designs.

Kimpston and Anderson (1982) in a study of curriculum planning in multiple school districts identified these tasks: determining areas needing revision, formulating overall philosophy and goals, selecting subject matter objectives/content/sequence, selecting curriculum materials, setting student expectations, among others.

Short (1983) studied numerous cases of curriculum development and detected three types of strategies being used where decisions among substantive options are based on criteria of purposefulness, practicality, realism, and judiciousness.

Orpwood (1985, 297) noted that curriculum development sets "rules, plans, or guides for what shall be taught in a specific situations" through processes of deliberation.

Ben-Peretz and Tamir (1986, 11) noted that a planning team "decided on basic aims, content, and the general framework" and a working team "decided on operational objectives, student activities, format, sequence, time allocation, and content areas to be emphasized," as well as curriculum materials and evaluation procedures to be used. Both group deliberation and solitary drafting of curriculum packages were evident.

Boersma and Looy (1997), in the Netherlands, produced a theory of curriculum development in which a mix of practical knowledge and theoretical knowledge is used to arrive at decisions on guidelines for curriculum plans and implementation.

Visscher-Voerman (1999), also in the Netherlands, studied twenty-four cases of curriculum development and found four models operating: planning by objectives (starting with outcomes and reasoning back to a product); a sociopolitical process to reach consensus; building prototype designs, trying them out and revising them repeatedly until a satisfactory result is reached; and creation of a product in response to a specific situation (an artistic/connoisseurship model).

Chen et al. (2015) found that conversation, negotiation, and compromise were commonly employed with both internal and external stakeholders during school-based curriculum development in six Singapore schools.

we to make of such differing conceptions? Which is the most accurate depiction of what should be said and done in conducting curriculum practice? Does this list include the candidate for the best definition of curriculum practice? Or is such a definition yet to be devised? On what basis is a viable definition of curriculum practice to be stipulated?

In preparation for attempting to address these questions, we will begin by categorizing and analyzing the conceptions of curriculum practice listed in boxes 3.2 and 3.3. Table 3.1 lists eleven groupings of specific concepts and actions mentioned by these authors, classified by key operational

Table 3.1. Classifications of Conceptions of Curriculum Practice

By Key Operational Concept	Authors
Making Decisions	Tyler (1949); Herrick (1950); Taba (1962); Goodlad (1979); Eisner (1979)
Following Fixed Procedures	Taba (1962); Johnson (1967); Klein & Goodlad (1979); Walker (1979); Wilson (1979); Eible & Zavarella (1979); Kimpston & Anderson (1982); Steller (1983); Ber-Perez & Tamir (1986); Visscher-Voerman (1999)
Pursuing Problem Solving Strategies	Tanner & Tanner (2007); Westbury (2008)
Solving-Problems by Practical Judgment	Reid (1978); Short (1983)
Outlining a Plan	Skilbeck (1982); Ben-Perez & Tamir (1986); Visscher-Voerman (1999)
Using Design Principles	Eraut (1990); Visscher-Voerman (1999); van den Akker (2010)
Implementing Policy	Eible & Zavarella (1979); Eisner (1979); Wilson (1979); Westbury (2008)
Negotiating Consensus	Goodlad (1979); Gay (1984); Visscher-Voerman (1999); Westbury (2008); Chen (2015)

continued on next page

Table 3.1. Continued

By Key Operational Concept	Authors
Utilizing Curriculum Expertise	Boorsman & Looy (1997); Kunzli in Rosenmund (2002)
Creating Guidelines for Enactment of a Plan	Macdonald (1986)
Conducting Deliberations	Schwab (1969); Walker (1971); Reid (1978); Orpwood (1985); Ben-Perez & Tamir (1986); Macdonald & Purpel (1987); Biesta (2013)

Nonitalicized authors are those whose conceptions of curriculum practice were based on their personal experience.

Italicized authors are those whose conceptions of curriculum practice were based on research.

concept and labeled in a way intended to embrace the various expressions of that concept that were identified within each grouping. Beside each category are listed those authors whose conceptions of curriculum practice were identified as falling within that category.

The first category listed suggests that operationally curriculum practice can be conceived primarily as a matter of *making decisions*. This notion can hardly be contested, since decisions of many kinds have to be made in putting together a plan for curriculum. The problem with this way of defining the essence of curriculum practice, however, would appear to be that it does not state exactly what the decisions are that must be made and, therefore, does not provide much clarity as to what must be said or done in the process of making these decisions. The examples mentioned by authors in this category frequently say: take this, take that, take a number of things into account when making curriculum decisions and put them together to come up with a plan. Just how all this is to be done is left open; it can seem to be quite complex and mind-boggling and begs for additional guidance. I conclude that curriculum practice cannot be operationally defined in a helpful way as making decisions.

Following fixed procedures is another way curriculum practice has been attempted to be defined operationally. This conception has a considerable history of application as evidenced by the numerous authors associated with this category and the fact that several listed in other categories often encourage the use of this approach as well. Although they differ in the number and identity of steps they suggest should be followed, these authors tend to agree that their procedures should be focused on making decisions regarding a set of basic curriculum topics that makes up a curriculum plan (they may differ on what these topics are). Since a diverse array of "fixed procedures" is espoused by different authorities, curriculum practitioners are forced to choose which procedures to follow. Consequently, this conception of curriculum practice leads to multiple forms of curriculum practice rather than to a conception that is universally applicable and capable of defining the essential nature of curriculum practice. The chances of reaching an agreement across authorities on which of the steps and topics to use seems unlikely. Therefore, following fixed procedures does not appear to be a reliable way of defining what is to be said and done in curriculum practice.

Pursuing problem-solving strategies is a third way of conceiving curriculum practice operationally. The authors in this category do not give much in the way of precise guidance on how to conduct problem solving in the context of curriculum planning. Perhaps the assumption is that everyone knows what problem solving requires (such as, identify a problem, devise a solution that fits the circumstances, evaluate its feasibility and/or devise another solution, and make a determination to proceed with implementation of the solution). The pursuit of problem-solving strategies implies that there are many ways to accomplish problem solving, and therefore, it is necessary to identify which conception of problem solving to pursue before one can proceed. Consequently, this approach suffers from the same limitation as that associated with following fixed procedure—its nonuniversality. In addition, in any problem-solving approach, one must begin with a problem; not everything that needs to be said and done in curriculum practice can be stated in the form of a problem to be solved. Making decisions on various matters is perhaps more typical than casting everything as problems to be solved. Conceiving of curriculum practice as pursuing problem-solving strategies would appear to be problematic and less than operationally ideal.

Solving problems by practical judgment is another conception of curriculum practice found on the list. This is a variation on the previous category. It has the advantage of specifying the particular way of doing problem solving that is to be used. Practical judgment entails offering reasons for the ways one chooses to recommend the solutions to the problems being addressed, weighing alternative arguments, and coming to considered agreements on the solution recommended. While this approach may not be as specific as one might wish in providing "how-to-do-it" aspects of engaging in practical judgment, it does not require a search for which way to do problem solving; it specifies the use of practical judgment. Still, it is necessary that a problem be identified as the starting point in this approach, and therefore, it suffers from the same concern as noted for problem-solving strategies in general. I conclude that this conception of curriculum practice does not epitomize what is truly basic to the nature of curriculum work.

The next key operational concept listed in table 3.1 is *outlining a plan* for a curriculum. Who can argue with this one? Surely, all of the conceptions categorized in table 3.1 imply this as "a" task of curriculum practice if not "the" entire task. The problem with this is that it is so general that it is really not helpful at all in defining what is to be said and done in curriculum practice. What to do and how to do it are missing.

Using design principles is most often employed in curriculum projects where revision of plans, products, or materials is sought, rather than for initial development. This approach provides a way of trying out prototype plans, obtaining feedback, and deciding whether the desired specifications originally sought have been met, and if not, revising them, re-implementing them, checking the results again against original specifications, and following this cycle over and over until the desired result is obtained. This approach follows a research and development model in which the techniques of design technology and rigorous data-based revision are utilized. It is not appropriate for devising a curriculum for the first time (or for revising programs), where there cannot be a set of specifications identified in advance. Drafting a curriculum does not involve knowing the ultimate outcome of the plan; it only states what is prescribed or desired. While there may be criteria adopted in advance for what a curriculum plan should deal with or look like in its completed form, these criteria cannot serve as specifications for what the results of its implementation should be, whereas in design technology the desired result is known in advance and successive iterations of plans can be drafted until the specified results are obtained. Using design principles cannot be the key concept in curriculum practice where creating a plan for curriculum requires originating ideas and actions rather than adjusting plans or products to ideal specifications.

Implementing policy is a natural activity inherent in creating curriculum plans. Curriculum practitioners ordinarily take policy statements made by governing agencies with which they are associated (school boards, legislatures, sponsors of nongovernmental education entities, etc.) and translate them into practical programmatic plans designed to actualize the desired policy statements. But to say that implementing policy is the key activity of curriculum practice is to say very little about what they must actually say and do in order to fulfill their obligation to policy makers. Policy implementation work at the level of curriculum planning requires a lot of specific activities for which this concept provides no operational help at all.

Negotiating consensus sometimes occurs in doing curriculum work when political or ideological differences among the individuals involved preclude ready agreement on specific decisions. Negotiating these differences is most often required in connection with determining basic assumptions and value preferences on which other curriculum decisions are made, rather than for a majority of the decisions concerned with the other components of curriculum. In fact, many of the decisions requiring the negotiation of political or ideological differences occur during curriculum policy debates rather than during curriculum planning activities. Most of the work involved in developing curriculum plans requires thinking more akin to logical reasoning, rather than compromise on differences of opinion and consensus building. Agreement in the realm of determining what will be consistent from one part of a curriculum plan to another is much easier to attain (by recasting the parts that don't hang together) than agreement on basic assumptions and values that are to undergird a curriculum. It is, therefore, not correct to say that the key operational concept that pervades curriculum practice is negotiating consensus even though this may occur at times.

Utilizing curriculum expertise certainly is part of curriculum practice. If curriculum practitioners are to accomplish their work successfully, they need to have (or to acquire) several kinds of expertise, for example, subject matter knowledge from which suitable content can be selected. They also need to how to structure the content chosen, how to arrange allocations of time and students to fit the parameters of the program organization chosen, how to express the decisions made in all aspects of the curriculum plan in practical, understandable terms for those who must enact the plan, how to work collegially within the group doing curriculum planning, and so forth. But just to state that curriculum practitioners must have and use this sort of expertise does not provide helpful guidance for doing so. The participants in the process still have to figure out what particular expertise is required, when and how to use it, and how to acquire it in the first place. This cannot be the concept that provides the key to what is to be done in curriculum practice.

Creating guidelines for enactment of a plan—this, too, is part of engaging in the work of curriculum practice; however, it is not the key activity of this work. A well-planned curriculum outline will contain information on how it is to be enacted, as we have already said, in terms that are understandable and doable. But the primary product of the work of curriculum practitioners is a curriculum plan itself, and whatever is required to attain that product is the key activity of curriculum practice, not the ancillary work of creating guidelines for its enactment.

Conducting deliberations, the last of the eleven categories extracted from the definitions of curriculum practice given by the several authors cited above, is, in my judgment, the key operational concept involved in what goes on in curriculum practice. Given that the preceding ten concepts do not convey adequately the central task that curriculum practitioners must perform, it remains for me to argue that *conducting deliberations* is that key operational concept. Deliberation, as defined by the authors cited in this category, (to paraphrase) is that activity in which options are considered, argued for and against, and chosen by persuasion (not compromise). In the context of curriculum planning, this activity and the thought processes involved occur with every single decision to be made in prescribing the plan for a curriculum—all those pertaining to each of the ten components that constitute curriculum as stipulated previously, and to each of the many subchoices that may be made within each of these ten components. I discern from my experience with curriculum planning that everything that is to be decided in planning a curriculum can be accomplished by engaging in this process of conducting deliberations. This cannot be accomplished by any of the ten activities listed before this one in table 3.1, for reasons stated in my analyses in the preceding paragraphs.

Rather than making curriculum plans by means of any of these other limited or faulty processes, the process of deliberation allows for the following highly desirable ideals to function: (1) full democratic participation by all members engaged in curriculum practice; (2) the best planning is done closest to the students who are to be affected by the plan; (3) even so, the process (and vocabulary) is the same at every level of curriculum planning (local, district, state, or nation), thereby making transactional activities from one level to another easier; (4) keeps curriculum work independent of biases and perspectives of participants and special interests; (5) the professional preparation of curriculum practitioners should focus exactly on what defines the work they are to do; (6) curriculum planning is a moral enterprise rather than a highly linear or deductive one; (7) curriculum planning should be so open and general that any conceivable version of a prescribed curriculum can be accommodated by its procedures and processes. Arguments made above in analyzing the concepts in table 3.1 provide evidence that the process of deliberation is consistent with these seven ideals, while the other conceptions are not.

More could be said to demonstrate the appropriateness of adopting *conducting deliberations* as the key operational concept in curriculum practice (and more will be said about this later in this chapter), but for now with this conception in mind let us revise the tentative definition of curriculum practice that was stated earlier in this chapter, prior to our analysis of published definitions. That tentative definition is restated here for convenient reference. *Curriculum practice is defined as the series of sayings and doings that is involved in prescribing the preferred conceptions and actions for all ten curriculum components that persons conducting curriculum practice must engage in if the intended purposes of this practice are to be accomplished.*

I wish to revise this statement in light of recognizing that the key operational concept in curriculum practice is conducting deliberations.

> *Curriculum practice is stipulated to be a series of deliberations on the preferred conceptions and actions to be prescribed in a particular curriculum plan (addressing all ten components of a complete curriculum) and the formulation of the resulting preferences in clearly specified prescriptions of the conceptions and actions that are to be enacted.*

Further consideration of the role this definition of curriculum practice is to play in a grammar of curriculum practice will follow in the next chapter, which addresses how a grammar of curriculum practice is to be conceived.

The definition of curriculum practice stipulated here contains some terms and expressions that need to be analyzed more fully so that functional concepts related to each of them can be identified, labeled (named), and defined more precisely. These still somewhat ambiguous terms and expressions are: *deliberations, preferred conceptions and actions, and formulation of prescriptions.* The other major terms within this definition, *curriculum, the ten components of curriculum,* and *practice,* have previously been given precise labels and definitions in earlier chapters and need no further attention here.

Deliberations

First, consider the concept of *deliberation* and what a series of deliberations might look like. Earlier it was noted that Schwab (1969) first brought the concept of deliberation to the attention of curriculum scholars and practitioners. He presented this overview of the concept of deliberation.

> Deliberation is complex and arduous. It treats both ends and means and must treat them as mutually determining one another. It must try to identify, with respect to both, what facts may be relevant. It must try to ascertain the relevant facts in the concrete case. It must try to identify the desiderata in the case. It must generate alternative solutions. It must make every effort to trace the branching pathways of consequences which may flow from each alternative and affect desiderata. It must then weigh alternatives and their costs and consequences against one another,

and choose, not the right alternative, for there is no such thing, but the best one. (Schwab, 1969, 36)

A number of other curriculum writers have also sought to describe what is involved in deliberation and its role in curriculum practice.[2] A review of these definitions will be helpful in trying to identify what is entailed in carrying out this process. The specific operational concepts they identify as inherent in this process are either quoted in box 3.4 or described in précis form in parentheses following some of the quotations.[3]

> **Box 3.4**
> **Descriptions of Deliberation by**
> **Various Curriculum Experts**
>
> "The main operations in curriculum deliberation are formulating decision points, devising alternative choices at these decision points, considering arguments for and against suggested alternatives, and choosing the most defensible alternative subject to acknowledged constraints" (Walker, 1971, 54).
>
> "Deliberation or practical reasoning is an intricate and skilled intellectual and social process whereby we identify the questions to which we must respond, establish grounds for deciding on answers, and then choose among the available solutions" (Reid, 1978, 43). (Reid emphasized that practical reasoning involves making moral and value judgments of public significance, justifying them in their institutional context, and determining a course of action to be taken. Elsewhere Reid provided further elaboration on how practical reasoning should function in curriculum work; see Reid 1988 and 1999, ch. 3.)
>
> "[Curriculum deliberation involves] the identification of the places where change is wanting, the borrowing or invention of alternative ways of fulfilling identified wants, deliberation on the costs and benefits of these alternatives, and, at last, their initiation with convinced and ready teachers . . . for

the relative weighting of the commonplaces which is appropriate to this time and place" (Schwab, 1983, 244). (Schwab identified the commonplaces referred to in this definition as teacher, student, what is taught, milieu of teaching-learning, and curriculum-making. Additional comments on the role of deliberation in curriculum practice are included in this source as well.)

"Use the arts of perception, problemation, prescription, and commitment to perform certain tasks" (Pereira, 1984, 338–389). (These tasks would include specifying symptoms of a problem [perceiving the problem], establishing reasons for this state of affairs [situation analysis], stating the problem, inventorying resources and constraints, generating a plan of action, rehearsing the consequences of proposed action, and deliberating the final choice of action to be taken.)

"Deliberations designed to formulate a curriculum policy must be regarded as having two dimensions: a rational dimension and a political dimension. . . . At the first stage of deliberations, contributions, whether facts, principles, or specific proposals, are collected and tested for their relevance. Those that are seen to be relevant become considerations and receive further deliberation. The second stage consists of weighing considerations to determine reasons 'on balance' for acting in a particular way. The conclusions then show the practical argument concluded and the political problem resolved" (Orpwood, 1985, 298, 301).

"[Deliberation is] a systematic method for individuals, groups, or institutions to formulate and entertain an adequate variety of alternatives—alternative perceptions and formulations of problems in situations and alternative solutions—directed toward decisions about what and how to teach particular students in a particular context. . . . [It takes the form of] perceiving the relevant details in a situation, generating alternative formulations of the problem(s), generating alternative solutions, and acting upon the best one, not the right one, all things considered. . . . It involves both reality and value judgments, negotiating among morally engaged individuals interacting in the setting of social institutions" (Harris, 1991, 295, 297–298).

"[The activities of deliberation include] depiction of a problematic situation, alternative formulations of likely solutions, forecasting their consequences, weighing them against purposes and anticipated satisfactions, and choosing a solution and enacting it" (Dillon, 1994, 17).

"[Phases in the process of deliberation include] public sharing of possible actions, highlighting of agreements and disagreements, explaining positions, highlighting changes in position, negotiating points of agreement, and adopting a decision" (Noye, 1994, 240–242).

"Deliberators conceive a problem, create and weigh alternative solutions and actions, envision probable outcomes of each, consider means and ends/facts and values, and select or develop the best course of action" (McCutcheon, 1995, 4–5). (Deliberation has a moral dimension and has social responsibilities.)

"[Processes in deliberation through practical reasoning include] sensing a problem and stating it well, exploring potential courses of action, and choosing the best course of action" (Walker, 2003, 220–234). (This third process involves making arguments for and against each course of action and identifying principles and evidence to substantiate these arguments.)

In order to detect how much convergence exists among all these definitions, a categorization of the actions mentioned in each of them is displayed in table 3.2.

A quick look at the various ways these authors identify the constituent operations in deliberation reveals considerable convergence. Perhaps this should not be surprising since they

Table 3.2. Categories of Actions within Deliberation

	1	2	3	4	5
Walker (1971)	Formulate decision points	Devise alternative choices	Consider arguments for and against alternatives	Choose the most defensible alternative	
Reid (1978)	Identify questions to respond to	Identify possible answers	Establish grounds for deciding	Choose a solution	
Schwab (1983)	Identify where change is wanting	Borrow or invent alternatives	Deliberate costs and benefits of alternatives	Make choice appropriate to time and place	Initiate by convinced and ready teachers
Pereira (1984)	Conduct situation analysis	Generate plans of action	Rehearse consequences and deliberate choices	Make a choice	Make a commitment to act on choice
Orpwood (1985)		Collect proposals, facts, principles	Test for relevance; weigh reasons	Conclude on an action to take	

continued on next page

Table 3.2. Continued

	1	2	3	4	5
Harris (1991)	Entertain alternative formulation of problems	Entertain alternative formulation of solutions	Negotiate, judge best solution, all things considered	Decide what and how to teach	
Dillon (1994)	Depict the problem situation	Formulate likely alternative solutions	Weigh them against purposes and satisfactions	Choose a solution	Enact the solution
Noye (1994)		Share publicly possible actions	Negotiate agreements and dis-agreements	Adopt a decision	
McCutcheon (1995)	Conceive a problem	Create likely alternative solutions	Weigh probable results of each alternative	Select the best course of action	
Walker (2003)	Sense a problem and state it well	Explore potential courses of action	Make arguments for and against each course of action	Choose the best course of action	

tend to mimic the common understanding of the definition of deliberation—"a careful weighing of the reasons for or against something."

In my view, the actions listed in columns 1 and 5 of table 3.2 are not really part of the act of deliberation. Those listed in column 1 are activities that need to occur prior to engaging in deliberation, while those in column 5 need to occur after deliberation is completed. Both kinds of activities certainly need to be done, of course, but they need to be undertaken by other people charged with this work rather than by curriculum practitioners charged with doing just two basic activities inherent in doing curriculum work—deliberating and prescribing (as stipulated in our definition of curriculum practice). These are evident in the concepts listed in columns 2, 3, and 4.

I now wish to offer a more precise definition of deliberation—one conceived for use in conducting the work of curriculum practice by curriculum practitioners.

> *Deliberation is stipulated to consist of five actions required to reach a decision on any aspect of curriculum work, each of which is construed as follows:*
>
> *1. identify substantive options/alternatives/choices to be considered;*
>
> *2. state reasons why each option is or is not a desirable one;*
>
> *3. assess strengths and weaknesses of the arguments across options;*
>
> *4. identify the options for which the strongest arguments can be made;*
>
> *5. reach consensus on which option is the best, all things considered.*

Because deliberation is a group activity (several curriculum practitioners are involved), multiple options for any particular decision will surely be put forth as desirable as well as multiple reasons pro and con given for choosing them. Quite often, however, curriculum practitioners are unaware of possible options related to the substantive matters about which they are to make decisions (for the ten components of curriculum as stipulated in our definition of curriculum practice). In this case, they will need to seek to discover other possibilities in addition to those they may be able to identify on their own. While they may find it relatively easy to determine the best option among a narrow range of options, it is no doubt wiser to consider a broad range of options before making a decision if they wish to forestall quarrels over their decision by those who may find reasons to wonder if other options might have been better or for whom the reasons given for their choice do not seem persuasive enough. Time is well spent identifying and weighing a wide range of options.

The appeal to certain views of what might be seen as desirable in determining their preferences is key to assessing the strengths or weaknesses of the arguments made or rejected. Thus, the requirement to assess the arguments will force participants to articulate the basis for making and judging those arguments. These may be values and beliefs or they may be factual realities with which their arguments are meant to coincide or affirm. In any case, involved in these actions is the necessity of persuading members of the deliberative group of the virtue of the arguments presented until consensus on the best option is reached. Ultimately, the final arguments in support of the option chosen must be persuasive for those who are going to accept it and enact it.

The five constituent actions stipulated in this definition of deliberation are conceptualized in concrete operational terms, rather than in more general, perhaps vaguer terms, such as "assert your choices" without giving reasons or explaining why the choice was made, or just saying, "do some deliberation," however that might be interpreted by the participants. Each of the five actions stipulated is stated in unambiguous, easily understood terms that can readily be undertaken with a minimum of uncertainty about what is required. The set of five actions taken together constitutes what a complete act of deliberation entails as here construed. Nothing else is expected; nothing less will suffice.

The quality of the deliberations depends largely on who the deliberators are. Designation of the persons who are to engage in any particular deliberative occasion in curriculum work is, therefore, a very significant task. What expertise and experience they should bring to the activity of deliberation is a judgment to be made by those in authority who assign these persons to this task. It may depend on the scope of the work to be addressed. It may also depend on obtaining a balance among ideological or political perspectives held by members of the group being formed. Few governing authorities have stipulated certification requirements for those who engage in curriculum work, but if academically prepared and certified persons are available in the setting, they are prime candidates for this work. Ordinarily teachers and school leaders (sometimes assisted by student participants) frequently serve as curriculum practitioners, whether formally prepared for this task or not. In this case, they may need to be provided with expert assistance from more qualified persons who can help them gain access to needed expertise and related resources for their use. While the designation of persons to be entrusted with curriculum planning lies outside the domain of curriculum practice, it is of such importance for the achievement of the goals of curriculum practice that it cannot be handled casually or without consideration of the many factors that can affect the effectiveness of their work.

Deliberation is a purposeful action directed toward making decisions about some topic or issue that requires that a choice be made. In curriculum deliberations those matters are identified in our definition of curriculum practice as the ten components of curriculum. What are the options for each component and what are the arguments that favor a particular option among the various possibilities? This is the task of curriculum deliberation. Deliberation in any context must have something to deliberate; what the focus of deliberation is to be must be made clear to all who participate in the deliberation. That is why we have intentionally identified exactly what must be addressed in producing a curriculum plan (the ten components) so that what is to be addressed will be quite clear at the onset of curriculum deliberations. The uncertainty that sometimes exists in other forms of curriculum decision-making about what constitutes a curriculum plan, and, therefore, about what decisions are to be made, is replaced by a definite agenda for curriculum deliberation (the ten components).

Preferred Conceptions and Actions

Deliberation is the key activity undertaken in curriculum practice. But what are the objects of deliberation? What should the resulting decisions look like? For any particular component of curriculum (and for all ten of them), what precisely are the kinds of things about which preferences are to be sought? The content of the preferences, of course, are determined by the nature of the component being deliberated, such as the focus/purpose or the subject matter content of the curriculum. The form that such preferences should take will be discussed in the next section of this chapter. However, as stipulated in our definition of curriculum practice, they are of two types, *conceptions* and *actions*, and are the same across all components of curriculum. Let us analyze and elucidate these two terms.

In determining what is preferred among several alternatives for the choice of curriculum content (the substantive component), perhaps between blocks of humanities content versus separate disciplinary content, when the choice is finally agreed on, that choice needs to be identified, labeled, and defined in such a way as to be clearly understood. This is an example of a resulting preference that has to be stated *conceptually*. In structuring the curriculum, this choice has to be thought about and the content arranged in congruence with the definition of the preferred choice. On the other hand, if a choice is made that certain content be allocated to the elementary portion rather than to the secondary portion of the curriculum, this is an example of an *action* formulation of a choice. In structuring the curriculum, this choice has to be acted on, not conceptually, but practically, and laid out in the sequencing of the plan. Neither form is better than the other; it just depends on whether action or thought must be taken. Both types can and will be found among whatever preferences are stipulated. Some of the curriculum components lend themselves more toward one form or the other. In the assumptive component, for instance, conceptual type preferences are most likely. In the supportive arrangements component, action preferences are quite likely to be more often specified. But in the substantive component, as just illustrated, both conceptions and actions are possible and necessary.

These two categories of preferred outcomes of deliberation are of significance in curriculum practice for several reasons. Recall that in chapter 1, which dealt with "practice," it was recognized that both the discourse and the activities of practice were essential characteristics of a practice (both its sayings and its doings). Some of the work involves discourse and some if it involves taking action. Knowing when one or the other of these is required is part of understanding what must be done in a practice. When is choosing among conceptual objects the required task, and when is choosing among possible actions the required task? And how is one not to confuse one with the other? In the midst of deliberating among options, is it clear which type of outcome is being sought? In coming to a resolution on the best option among several options, is the deliberation focused on a conceptual matter or an actionable matter? And are the arguments in support of that option intellectual or practical, moral or prudential? These are the kinds of questions provoked by the circumstances and focus of deliberation and must be answered satisfactorily by the participants.

One could ask whether the objects of deliberation might be some other type, instead of or in addition to, those identified as conceptions and actions. What other possibilities might there be? Could giving examples or providing detailed descriptions of the chosen preferences be useful ways of presenting them? Would graphic displays or analytic categories suffice? Why are conceptions and actions really the best forms in which to specify preferences for all the components of a curriculum plan? An adequate response to these kinds of questions rests largely on what those who use the planned curriculum require for gaining a precise understanding of it and how it is meant to be enacted. Too much detailed description can sometimes lead to missing the essence of what is being prescribed. Spelling out too fully the formulation of what is intended can also leave too little flexibility in how the preferences can be tailored to fit particular circumstances. This is especially a problem considering a curriculum may cover twelve or more years of time and changing circumstances. Too little information, on the other hand, such as giving illustrative examples or condensed graphic depictions or listing of types of things, can lead to misinterpretations of or deviations from the intended preferences and thus can lead to imprecise understanding of the prescribed plan. The advantage of adopting conceptions and actions as the key operational forms for casting the results of deliberation is that they define precisely the kind of discourse and action that users can readily grasp and follow.

The term, *conceptions*, in our definition of curriculum practice refers to those abstract views of a matter being addressed that are meant to govern the kind of specific applications drawn from them. So, in our earlier example of curriculum content prescribed to be "blocks of humanities content" (as distinguished from other possible structured arrangements of content), specifying the desired structure requires that the conception of "blocks of humanities content" be named and explicitly defined in such a way that there is no confusion about what this way of structuring content allows and requires in organizing content over the time span of the curriculum covered by this prescription. The preferences of this type, conceptions, might conceivably be collapsed into the type here referred to as actions, where the action called for would be to implement the conception. However, this does not seem to qualify as an action in the same way that a direct specification of an action does, so conceptions are reserved as a different type of outcome of deliberation. Conceptions require some extended thinking about how they apply to a curriculum plan. While they do give focus and direction for what is planned, they do not specify immediate actions that are required. A plan will necessarily require tweaking in various ways if the conception is to be embodied in it appropriately. Vigilance will be required to detect whether the plan does in fact incorporate the conception as specified. It involves thinking, discourse, and making adjustments in the plan by the planners and enactors.

The term, *actions*, in our definition of curriculum practice refers to those specific activities that deliberators have identified should be carried out directly as they have presented them if the plan is to be designed and enacted as they envision it. They will indicate, "do this," "do that." For example, "spend year three on calculus," or "engage students in project learning," or "evaluate curriculum on a three-year cycle by subject areas." Again, these actions are to be stated as precisely as possible so that there is no confusion about what is intended. Actions are less likely to be misinterpreted than conceptions because actions can be stated quite directly and clearly. If latitude in an action is permitted, it should be clearly stated how much latitude is permitted. If an action is to be prohibited, that too should be specified. No specified action should contradict another specified action. It would seem prudent to present as many as possible of the outcomes of deliberation as actions rather than as conceptions; in this way, there is less room for curriculum planners and enactors to misconstrue the intentions of the deliberators and include or exclude something incorrectly.

In summary, I am persuaded that *conceptions* and *actions* are the appropriate forms that the results/outcomes of curriculum deliberations should take and wish to define them as follows: *Conceptions and actions are stipulated to be the only appropriate types of outcomes of curriculum deliberation, where conceptions are construed as ideational features and actions are construed as direct imperatives to act.*

Prescriptions

How, then, are the decisions made by means of deliberation to be presented? How should the preferred conceptions and actions that have been chosen and agreed on be formulated? My response to this question, as evident in the definition of curriculum practice stipulated in this book, is: *by means of issuing prescriptive statements*. How are these prescriptive statements to be formulated? What factors should be considered in determining how these statements are to be formulated? What key operational concepts can be employed to focus this activity and assure that the results are clear and functional for those who must enact these prescriptions? In attempting to deal with these and related questions, we need to address the third more-or-less ambiguous term in our definition of curriculum practice—*prescriptions*—and analyze, define, and elucidate what precisely is meant by *prescribing* in the context of curriculum planning.

To prescribe something, as commonly understood, is "to give a directive that has to be followed in a particular situation." This would appear at first glance to be a relatively clear and precise meaning for the term that needs no further elaboration. In the context of curriculum planning, however, as we have indicated, the question is apt to arise about how such a directive is to be stated. Even if a particular choice among alternative concepts and actions on a particular component of curriculum (or all components) has been determined through deliberation, is there a way of stating those concepts and actions (prescribing what is to be thought, said, or done) that will be as precise and useful as possible?

I find very little treatment of this matter in the literature of curriculum practice and scholarship, and so I am obliged to develop and affirm some new conceptual assistance in advancing a more precise understanding of what it means to prescribe something in the process of doing curriculum planning. I draw on work by Harris (1983, 1985), who notes four types of discourse available for use in formulating prescriptions for practice:

persuasive discourse, descriptive discourse, theoretical discourse, and use of "an ideal case." Each of these has certain limitations; a combination is potentially desirable. I have acknowledged the necessity of using persuasive discourse by stipulating that every component of curriculum requires the presentation of arguments and justification. In analyzing the other three options, I find all of them too complex and less well focused than is desirable for defining the sort of discourse required to communicate the concepts and actions prescribed for a curriculum plan. What I conclude is needed is an approach that is applicable to all decisions prescribed regardless of curriculum component and that is clear and easy to grasp and follow.

To illustrate the need and the problem, let us suppose, for example, that curriculum planners wish to prescribe as a long-range purpose for their curriculum the idea of "enabling students to flourish in life." How can this be made clear and actionable in directives they issue? As a way of beginning to think about a response to this question, I would first of all say that the statements issued should take the form of imperative sentences—as opposed to declarative ones or (less likely) interrogative sentences or exclamatory sentences—for example, "think this" or "do that." Give concrete ideas about what a flourishing life would be like—perhaps, "release one's potential gifts and talents," "thrive socially and civically," or "attain ever-increasing levels of maturity as a human being." Such assertions are not only more precise and more meaningful than simply stating, "enable students to flourish in life," but they also provide clearer directives on which to make choices in other parts of a curriculum (e.g., the subject matter choices, or unique prescriptions for the student transactive component).

Imperative sentences can embody the decisions coming out of deliberations and at the same time assist curriculum planners and enactors to grasp correctly what those decisions functionally imply for subsequent decisions and actions they will have to take. As another example, consider a decision on how to structure the substantive component of curriculum, for example, "general education is to be structured by integrated subjects rather than by separate disciplines." As stated, this is a declarative sentence, not an assertion of what to think or to do. What if this were stated as "fuse content from multiple disciplines by themes"? This formulation gives more precise meaning to "integrated subjects," which could be interpreted in many different ways, some of which might not have been intended by those making the decision on this matter. And it tells exactly how to integrate the subjects.

Imperative sentences are performative in nature (Austin, 1975, 6). They contain statements or utterances that signal actions to be taken. They employ action verbs. They command a specific kind of thought or action. Prescriptions, as construed in our definition of curriculum practice, would appear to be best expressed in imperative language—in discourse that uses specific action verbs to indicate what is intended. Imperative sentences can include both assertions of prescribed conceptions and assertions of prescribed actions. Assertions state something that is held firmly and desired. Both kinds of assertions can be labeled by the term, *directives*, and I choose to use the term *directives* as the key operational concept denoting the way curriculum prescriptions should be formulated. The term, *directive*, appears to be applicable across all components of curriculum and identifies more clearly than any other term the kind of statements that will most clearly communicate what is intended by whatever curriculum prescriptions have been decided on. Directives allow for a range of possibilities but set boundaries on what possibilities are permissible and also allows for choosing the most feasible option within what is prescribed by the directive. The term *directives* incorporates the characteristics of imperative sentences, and at the same time, it is more exact and avoids technical terminology. Everyone understands what issuing a directive means. I choose *directives* as the most appropriate way of formulating the results of curriculum deliberations and define this term as follows:

> *Directives are stipulated to be the most appropriate kind of statement in which to formulate the prescribed*

> *conceptions and actions resulting from curriculum deliberations, where a directive is construed as containing both a precise explanation of a particular prescribed conception or action that is to be implemented and a narrowly focused action verb(s) specifying what is to be said or done to implement that conception or action.*

A couple of expressions in this definition deserve comment. A directive contains two parts, an ideational component and an action component—the first represented by the phrase, "a precise explanation of a particular prescribed conception or action that is to be implemented," and second by the phrase "a narrowly focused action verb(s) specifying what is to be said or done to implement that conception or action." A particular directive will usually state what is to be done (the second component) about the first component. Choosing the action verbs may be less difficult than determining how to precisely and clearly state the ideational component, but they will go hand-in-hand and need to be seen as interdependent. Thinking of the "explanation" component as a directive (just as much as thinking of the action part as a directive) should make the formulation of the ideational component easier than if it were thought of in the usual sense of giving reasons.

In order to test the applicability of this definition to the ten components of a curriculum, I have composed some illustrative directives for each of the ten components and presented them in table 3.3.

In the process of doing this, I have sought to determine whether the definition is adequately functional in all ten instances. Notice that I have concluded that it is quite possible to formulate prescriptions in all of these instances by the means defined as directives, except for two components: the assumptive and the contextual realities components. The illustrations given for these two components in table 3.3 are not really formulated as directives with the requisite action verbs. I have actually

Table 3.3. Illustrative Directives for the Ten Components of Curriculum

The Intentional Component	Release one's potential gifts and talents, thrive socially and civically, attain ever-increasing levels of being human
The Organizational Component	Fuse content from multiple disciplines by themes; require specialty studies starting at year 10; devote ½ time daily to general studies and ¼ time each to specialty studies & to enrichment/exploratory education
The Substantive Component	Include scientific aspects of environmental studies within evolutionary studies of biology, include ethical aspects of environmental studies within civic education content, exclude theological treatments of the environment from both biology and civics
The Assumptive Component	Democratic practices are basic to social life and should be adhered to in all facets of schooling; knowledge is established both by disciplined inquiry and by personal experience; freedom of thought and opinion is a basic right of all persons; all persons must be treated equally as human beings
The Contextual Realities Component	Current youth culture is replete with social/cultural media to the point of ignoring much else; the students for whom the curriculum is planned is half white, a quarter black, a quarter Hispanic, all of lower socioeconomic status; an environmental and economic crisis faces both the local and worldwide community

The Student Transactive Component	Do laboratory/field activities in all science subjects; participate in choosing civic issues to study; present a culminating research paper, speech, or performance before graduating
The Teaching Transactive Component	Give no lecture of more than ten minutes (unless teaching listening skills or note taking); utilize inquiry approaches in small groups rather than large group direct instruction; provide differentiated approaches for all students, not just special needs students
The Evaluation Component	Gather data twice a year on how well the faculty think the organizational directives are working; visit classrooms regularly to detect whether the curriculum's unique purposes are being addressed; hold a yearly conference to consider changes needed in the planned curriculum
The Supportive Arrangements Component	Provide funding for field trips uniquely required by the curriculum; locate and schedule facilities/media use so that study time lost by students' moving from place to place is no more than five minutes; assign teachers to plan and teach in teams
The Justification Component	Present reasoning that explains why a particular directive is prescribed; state the rationale for how directives for various curriculum components interrelate and cohere; site the doctrine or the facts on which an argument is based

stated them in declarative sentences rather than in imperative sentences. I have tried to turn these assertions into directives, but I cannot really think of a way to do so. I believe the way assumptive prescriptions will have to be formulated (rather than as directives) is as *doctrines*; and I think contextual prescriptions will have to be formulated as *facts* or as statements of factual realities. Let us consider these alternatives for their possible merits.

Doctrines, in the context of education, can be said to "formulate persuasive rationalized systems of values or beliefs pertaining to the ends and means of educational practice" (Harris, 1985, 51). "Doctrines are typically justified by either sustained arguments or persuasive exhortations . . . but do not directly communicate the character of educational strategies" (Harris (1983, 37). Assumptive prescriptions for a curriculum, admittedly, do not include explicit strategies or actions to be taken, but they do include beliefs and/or values intended to affect the applicable curriculum plan in some part or in its totality. The concept, *doctrine*, appears to be exactly what a prescriptive assumption is, as stipulated as one of the ten components of curriculum. Defined in this way, a doctrine requires that its prescriptive content be formulated to give an explicit account of, and arguments for, a particular belief or value (or set of beliefs or values) intended to undergird selected decisions on other curriculum components in the prescribed curriculum plan.

I also find that if prescriptions for the contextual realities component of curriculum cannot be stated in the form of directives, they will need to be formulated as matters of *fact*, most certainly in the form of declarative sentences. Any particular declarative statement of fact should assert the prevailing state of affairs in some domain of contextual reality along with persuasive evidence of its empirical validity. Such matters of fact will be presented as a basis for certain decisions on other curriculum components in the prescribed curriculum plan, although, in and of themselves, they do not directly prescribe actions to be taken.

In accord with these two exceptions to the use of the concept of *directives* as the way to formulate all curriculum prescriptions, I am compelled to modify the earlier definition of how they should be formulated as follows:

> *Directives are stipulated to be the most appropriate kind of statement in which to formulate the prescribed conceptions and actions resulting from curriculum deliberations in all components of a curriculum, except for the assumptive and the contextual realities components, where, respectively, doctrines and factual statements are most appropriate;*
>
> *a directive is construed as a statement containing both a precise explanation of a particular prescribed conception or action that is to be implemented and a narrowly focused action verb(s) specifying what is to be said or done to implement that conception or action;*
>
> *a doctrine is construed as a statement containing an explicit assertion of, and arguments for, a particular belief or value (or set of beliefs or values) intended to undergird some other selected curriculum decision(s);*
>
> *a factual statement is construed as a statement containing an explicit description of the prevailing state of affairs in some domain of contextual reality, along with persuasive evidence of its empirical validity for use as a basis for making some other selected curriculum decision(s).*

Recall that earlier in this chapter we set out to analyze, clarify, and elucidate three somewhat vague or ambiguous expressions found in the definition of curriculum practice—*deliberations, preferred conceptions and actions,* and *formulations of prescriptions.* We have now completed this effort and wish to conclude with some summary reflections on curriculum practice, the way it has been defined here, the key concepts chosen to operationalize it, and why this conceptualization may be considered a valid way to facilitate future curriculum work.

The definition of curriculum practice stipulated earlier in this chapter is reproduced here for further reflection and comment, but slightly altered to include the concept of directives, as follows:

> *Curriculum practice is stipulated to be a series of deliberations on the preferred conceptions and actions to be prescribed in a particular curriculum plan (addressing all ten components of a complete curriculum) and the formulation of the resulting preferences in clearly specified directives for the conceptions and actions that are to be enacted.*

This way of defining curriculum practice, in my perception, more accurately states what goes on in curriculum practice in real settings than is true of other conceptualizations presented at the beginning of this chapter by various scholars of curriculum work. It also has several advantages over many of these other definitions. See box 3.5.

Let me note here, by way of summary, some general observations about curriculum work as a practice that can be seen when it is defined as we have done in this book.

Curriculum practice is not intrinsically a matter of design, although the term was used in the past as a rough metaphor for what was thought to be involved in curriculum work. Design implies obtaining a solution to a problem. Curriculum practice is not a matter of obtaining a solution to a problem or a set of problems (where a satisfactory solution must meet certain criteria or expectations). The work of curriculum practice is not directed toward meeting a set of criteria. Many versions of the results of curriculum practice are possible and permissible, depending on a number of factors impinging on the decisions being made.

Box 3.5
Advantages of Adopting the
Stipulated Definition of Curriculum Practice

- It is more complete by virtue of its stipulating both the kinds of decisions and actions that are to be taken and what they are to be about.

- It specifies a definite agenda of items for which explicitly stated prescriptions are to be made in planning a complete curriculum with all its constituent components.

- It stipulates the kinds of sayings and doings that characterize the actual conduct of curriculum practice by incorporating insights from the scholarly domain of philosophy of language and its relation to professional practice.

- In identifying the constituent tasks in conducting curriculum practice, it draws on firsthand perceptions of the phenomenon rather than theoretical propositions or perspectives from research about such phenomenon, as many other definitions of curriculum practice do.

- It does not require an overly rational process of decision making; its key operational concept, deliberation, can be undertaken by those with firm convictions yet who are open to persuasion by others.

- It places the concept of directives as the primary target of these deliberations and emphasizes that they are to be determined in situ by practical reasoning and persuasive arguments rather than by external imposition.

- It is amenable to the exigencies of the circumstances and constraints of the educational institution or setting for which the curriculum directives are to be issued and enacted.

Rather, curriculum practice is a normative enterprise of determining a set of intentions regarding a series of topics that makes up a curriculum, given a particular set of students, educators, and circumstances for which the curriculum is intended. The primary activity inherent in curriculum practice, therefore, is a series of group deliberations about what these intentions should be and how they should be configured in an actual situation. The resultant curriculum represents the best choices that can be agreed on at a given point in time under prevailing circumstances. The curriculum could have turned out to be different with different deliberators or at a different time or under different circumstances. The work of curriculum practice, therefore, is to create a curriculum by these means and to formulate it in such a way that it can be brought into existence, if only temporarily, until such time as a new curriculum is desired or required by changing demands, authorities, deliberative action, or circumstances.

Having identified and defined the constituent ingredients and key operational concepts of curriculum practice, we are now in a position to consider how they may be related to each other to provide meaningful discourse and action in the conduct of curriculum practice. The next chapter addresses this semantic problem by attempting to conceptualize *a grammar* of curriculum practice, the final key term that we indicated in the opening chapter needed to be defined and elucidated.

Chapter 4

How a Grammar of Curriculum Practice Is to Be Conceptualized

This chapter focuses on the development of a grammar of curriculum practice that is built around the definition of curriculum practice stipulated in the previous chapter. What is meant by the phrase, "a grammar of curriculum practice," and why is such a grammar necessary? How is it to be conceived? What shall it consist of? How can it be used? Is more than one version of a grammar of curriculum practice possible? Why, or why not? These and related questions will be addressed in the process of attempting to analyze and construct a viable grammar of curriculum practice.

To begin, the concept of "a grammar" must be clearly understood and defined. Dictionary definitions of the term *a grammar* state that it refers to the ways words are combined in sentences to express meaning. It is concerned with discerning how language functions (Wittgenstein, 1968; de Saussure, 1986). Philosophers of language and scholars of linguistics refer to three dimensions of how language functions: its syntax, its semantics, and its pragmatics (Morris, 1938; Searle, 1970; Austin, 1975; Kemp, 2018). Syntax refers to rules of combining words into sense-making units. I quote the interpretation given to the term *syntax* by Jones (2002, 7): "The syntax of a language is the structure of relations among locutions in their use of signs."

Locutions are the phrases or expressions that contain words (signs) structured in particular ways to convey meaning. For example, "boy eats love" makes no sense, but "boy loves to eat" does. A syntactical rule applies here. Semantics refers to how signs (words) refer to a referent. Semantic rules give us ways to categorize and distinguish the objects referred to by given words. Since multiple referents are sometimes referred to by the same word, semantics is not "an exact science" and depends a great deal on the community of language within a given context of usage. Pragmatics refers to what is being accomplished whenever language is being used. It refers to the "intentions, actions, feelings, interests, agreements, and social practices" (Jones, 2002, 8) being activated by the locutions and signs used (language). The full functioning of language involves the interaction of all three dimensions of language—its syntax, its semantics, and its pragmatics.

A grammar, therefore, must be based on the following assumptions (derived from Jones, 2002, 17–18, based on the literature of the philosophy of language and of linguistics): (1) locutions to make sense are embedded in traditions of usage; (2) language has to be learned; (3) language provides the structure of our experience, understandings, and perspectives; (4) in language networks we learn the discourses and practices that comprise the world we see and discern; (5) the limits of language limit understanding of the world; (6) language is a human construct and construal (words do not have independent meanings); (7) we cannot step outside of language and look at the world; (8) our humanity is shaped by language; (9) grammar of language is a description of how human language makes sense in three ways—syntactic, semantic, and pragmatic; and (10) learning any human practice is to learn the language of its discourses and practices.

These assumptions interpreted within the realm of curriculum practice require that certain assumptions on which a grammar of curriculum practice rests be acknowledged at the outset and explicitly stated as follows: (1) associated with doing curriculum work are a set of activities (here labeled *curriculum practices*) that is essential to accomplishing that work in a real situation; (2) these activities collectively make up the practice of curriculum (here labeled *curriculum practice*); (3) curriculum practice is understood to be a type of human activity (practice) that involves (like all human practices) understanding and using specialized knowledge and experience pertaining to the essential tasks inherent in the practice to accomplish those tasks; (4) persons who engage in curriculum practice (here labeled *curriculum practitioners*) can be taught and learn to use the specialized knowledge and experience associated with curriculum practice in the process of accomplishing the essential tasks; (5) curriculum practitioners employ their specialized knowledge and experience by engaging in certain discourses and practices necessary to the conduct of their practice; (6) these specialized discourses and practices constitute the language of curriculum practice and are the object of this effort to set forth its grammar (here labeled *a grammar of curriculum practice*); (7) such a grammar of curriculum practice involves explicating the functioning of its language according to its syntax (its terms, words, and signs and the logic of their relationships), semantics (meanings given to these terms and relationships as they refer to particular subject matter), and pragmatics (interpretations attributed to these locutions in a given context of usage).

For purposes of this effort to construct a grammar of curriculum practice, our focus will be on the semantic dimension of language. (The syntax involved is assumed to be the same as that of language in general; the pragmatics involved is dependent on the way the language of curriculum practice is employed by its practitioners, which can be experienced by them as they work and can be studied by researchers interested in their language practices.) The vocabulary or terms that are unique to doing curriculum work, however, as we have seen, are crucial to any conceptualization of a grammar of curriculum practice. The effort to identify the key operational concepts involved in curriculum and in curriculum practice, and to give them precise labels (words with definite meanings), is a major focus of elucidating a grammar of curriculum practice. In addition, attention must be given to the way these concepts are related to one another in meaningful locutions and extended statements.

A definitive, comprehensive grammar of curriculum practice does not exist. If one existed, it could serve, as any grammar does, to facilitate an understanding and use of the discourse and activity (what is said and done) in curriculum practice. Elements of grammar help us state what it is we are talking about and are doing. It provides a backbone for conversations on these elements where differing viewpoints and perspectives may be taken and argued about. The set of key concepts established by a grammar of curriculum discourse and practice provides the foci around which differing viewpoints and perspectives can be offered and their merits (or demerits) can be assessed. At heart, a grammar of curriculum discourse and practice defines the inherent substance of what we are talking about or are doing, and how we go about expressing this in a particular context or milieu.

Many attempts to standardize the language of curriculum practice (its key concepts and practices) have been made historically. These attempts have necessarily failed because anyone can create such language, and inevitably, a great many people have done so in order to cast curriculum work as they perceive it or wish it to be perceived and used by others. However, standardization of the language of curriculum practice should not be the goal. Rather, the goal should be to identify and employ only those concepts that are constitutive of curriculum practice in a universal sense and allow a variety of alternative options in delineating specific preferences among aspects of curriculum and curriculum practices. A grammar of curricular language will incorporate these universal concepts into a structure of intelligible and meaningful language practices by which curriculum practice can be conducted with the least ambiguity in communication among curriculum practitioners and others who must understand and enact their prescribed plans. Such a grammar will specify and elucidate how these key concepts are interrelated and structured to form a viable language for use in conducting curriculum practice and related work.

To address this major facet of a grammar of curriculum practice, we need to recall that semantics is concerned with the relation between and among concepts employed in communicative discourse. Let us review the various concepts stipulated in this book that play a role in the language of curriculum practice and in constructing a prescribed curriculum plan. They have been identified as (1) concepts regarding the components constituting a curriculum, and (2) concepts regarding the constituent operations involved in conducting curriculum practice. So let us examine more closely these key concepts and the structure of their relationships as they are identified in our stipulated definition of curriculum practice, reproduced here for easy reference.

> *Curriculum practice is stipulated to be a series of deliberations on the preferred conceptions and actions to be prescribed in a particular curriculum plan (addressing all ten components of a complete curriculum) and the formulation of the resulting preferences in clearly specified directives for the conceptions and actions that are to be enacted.*

This definition contains four components of curriculum practice for which key concepts are identified: its *task, what is to be prescribed*, the *process* by which these decisions are to be made, and the *resulting products* of this process. The focal task of curriculum practice is identified by the key concept, "prescribing a curriculum plan." The component, what is to be prescribed, is defined by those decisions required by virtue of what a curriculum consists of (its ten components in table 2.4), namely, "what is to be prescribed for each and every component of curriculum." The key concept pertaining to the process by which these decisions are to be made is that of "deliberation." And the key concept defining what is to result from these deliberations is "the formulation of directives for thought and action."

In terms of what was earlier stated about the need to identify the semantic relationships among concepts employed in communicating clear and precise meanings, it is now necessary to identify and explain the nature of the relationships that should exist between and among the key operational concepts incorporated in our definition of curriculum practice and stipulated in connection with each of the four components of curriculum practice.

The task of *prescribing a curriculum plan* is assumed to be the focus and target of the work to be done in the conception of curriculum practice stipulated in this book. Other possible tasks have been relegated to other forms of educational practice for action in those realms. The task for curriculum practitioners is to prescribe a curriculum for a particular educational setting, not to propose one for a hypothetical situation or for academic or theoretical speculation or for some other purpose. In this basic concept, we have a relatively clear and unambiguous conception of the task to be accomplished and one that can serve as the basis for what is to be done in the other three components of curriculum practice.

What is to be prescribed is clearly identified by the concept stipulating that decisions are to be taken on all ten components of curriculum that constitute a complete curriculum and, consequently, must be set forth in an actual curriculum plan. Obviously, prescriptions for each component of curriculum and for all ten components (table 2.4) must be integrated into the final plan. They need to be related in some identifiable way. As was asserted earlier in this book, they cannot be related by logic. That is, the relation between components is not that of one component determining or implying the next in some prespecified order, and not even that any particular component's relationship with some other particular component is determined or implied by that component. Since these prescriptions are arrived at independently by deliberation, the relationships between and among them cannot be determined by deduction or by inference. They are not logical relationships. Rather, the relationships among the components of curriculum are, in all instances, ones of *consistency* and *noncontradiction*. That is, the language used to convey the meanings and actions prescribed in the directives for each component must be consistent with the language used in every other component, and they must not contradict one another. These same relationships must prevail for decisions within a particular component where prescriptions are set forth for any one or several subtopics. So as topics related to the ten components of curriculum are addressed, consideration must be given in all instances to making decisions that are consistent and noncontradictory with one another.

Deliberation is specified as the basic process by which curriculum decisions are to be made. It occurs over time for each topic addressed and consists of several phases (identifying options, stating reasons for desirability, assessing arguments for and against, choosing options with strongest arguments for, and reaching consensus on best option). Internally, these phases are *temporally* related but they are not often taken in linear order as listed. Moving back and forth from one phase to another is common, perhaps multiple times before consensus is reached. Deliberation is accomplished, not by some process of logic but by practical reasoning and argumentation. Across instances of deliberation on various components of curriculum, there must be a consciousness of the need for the decisions to be complementary and *consistent and noncontradictory*.

In addition, deliberation is *action-related*. It occurs because something must be decided in real time. Avoiding coming to a decision or procrastinating for whatever reasons are not expected activities associated with deliberation. The assigned task of prescribing a curriculum plan is vested in an action-oriented situation where decisions on all components of curriculum are required by the very nature of the assignment; some plan must be arrived at so that its enactment can be instituted. Without a plan, no curriculum can be activated.

Practicality is also characteristic of deliberation. What is decided through deliberation must be doable in the circumstances for which the curriculum plan is to be enacted and operationalized. A sense of the realities of the situation must be kept in mind as decisions are made. Prescribing something that cannot feasibly be acted on with reasonable assurance that it can be accomplished must be considered untenable and prohibited. *Fittingness* is also a relationship to be adhered to when making curriculum decisions, especially with regard to consideration of who the students are for whom the curriculum is being planned.

In the fourth component of the definition of curriculum practice, the key operational concept is *formulating directives for thought and action*. How are the directives arrived at as the result of deliberation to be related to one another and to other components of curriculum practice? The short answer is: by the already mentioned relationships of *consistency, noncontradiction, temporality, action-orientation, practicality, and fittingness*. All of these should be acknowledged in prescribing the directives for all conceptions and actions to be included in a curriculum plan. However, since all the directives prescribed must be combined into a single unified plan, it is important to examine further the relationships among directives as they take their place in a completed version of a curriculum plan. Here the language formulations employed require some complex semantic considerations beyond those concerned with individual directives. Analysis of semantic relationships in both individual directives and in combined sets of directives will be addressed in the next few paragraphs.

Semantic Analysis and Construction of Individual Directives

As stated previously, a directive is the basic linguistic form to be prescribed in a curriculum plan (which in its entirety is made up of a multiplicity of directives). A directive is the result of a decision about what to prescribe for a particular aspect of one of the curriculum components that constitutes a curriculum as stipulated in table 2.4. A single directive takes the form of an imperative sentence having two parts: an ideational component and an action verb. This sentence is usually accompanied by a statement(s) explaining and justifying the directive, but the basic prescription is communicated by this two-part formulation in an imperative sentence. The full meaning that the directive intends to communicate is conveyed by the semantic relationship that exists between these two parts. The action verb conveys what action is to be taken about the matter specified in the ideational component. Specifying one without the other does not suffice. Simply stating, for example, that a subject matter prescription (related to the substantive component) shall be Euclidean geometry as opposed to, say, algebra 2 does not tell us in actionable terms what is intended. An explicit choice of an appropriate action verb has to be specified and related to that substantive matter in order to communicate precisely what is intended by that prescription. So, an adequate directive for this example, using a precise action verb and delineating the content more precisely, might be stated as follows: "Place the study of theorems and postulates prior to the study of differential equations." Notice that using the word *prior* leaves considerable flexibility as to exactly where this content should be "placed," but at the same time, "placed prior to" clearly prescribes a required order for these two subject matter topics.

Semantically speaking, what is required in stating a directive is that the two parts must be related meaningfully. If the concepts contained in the ideational component make no sense when acted on in the way the action verb prescribes, even if they are properly stated syntactically, then something must be revised—either the ideas or the action verb or perhaps both. One would not prescribe, for example, "hold free play recess during science laboratory activities." The referent of the concept "free play recess" and referent of the concept "science laboratory activities" preclude the first from being "held during" the second. A principle of noncontradiction applies in constructing meaningful imperative statements, where some real action is required and where we are not engaging in speaking or writing imaginative or hypothetical discourse.

The Meaningful Structure of a Combined Set of Directives

When a whole set of directives are combined in a fully prescribed curriculum plan, the resulting structure of meaningful relationships among directives is considerably more complex than the semantic structure of individual directives. So how can these relationships be made evident when presenting a total set of curriculum directives? What is the appropriate language through which this product of deliberation and prescribed conceptions and actions should be communicated? How are the various prescriptions to be brought together and related to one another in such a way that the complete plan successfully communicates what the prescribers intended? What criteria can be applied to the semantic structure of the entire plan to assure that these intentions are clearly and accurately understood as a whole as well as in every part?

The task of bringing together all of the directives to be included in a particular curriculum plan is indeed a problem of language. It is not, however, one that can be accomplished by formula, logic, or external direction, or by merely listing them in some kind of predetermined sequence. It involves considerable creativity and practical judgment. A number of configurations may be appropriate depending on the circumstance in which the plan is to be received and enacted. What can be said that is applicable generally in all instances is that certain relationships among the statements presented must exist so that the overall semantic structure attains clarity of meaning and integral unity.

The directives for each and every component of curriculum are arrived at independently through the process of moral deliberation. They are placed together in a complete prescribed curriculum plan structured to be an integral whole in which all parts are consistent and noncontradictory. This construction of a complete curriculum plan that integrates all the prescribed directives is not accomplished by processes of logic but, in contradistinction, by methods more akin to those of artistic design. The elements are placed together (composed) in meaningful ways with respect to one another so that the various elements are understood to be mutually supportive and structurally unified. The language in which these prescriptions are expressed should convey not only what is intended in the way of ideas and actions but also what the relationships among them are intended to be. These intentions need to be expressed in precise enough language with sufficiently clear explanations that no element communicates any contradictory message to that communicated in some other part of the curriculum plan and that they are consistent with one another throughout the plan. If any one of these directives (or a number of them) is found to be inconsistent or contradictory with some other directive(s), then more deliberation needs to take place in order to come up with a directive(s) on that topic that is compatible with the others and that meets these criteria.[1]

In bringing together the full set of prescribed directives into a complete curriculum plan, in addition to assuring that they are mutually *consistent and noncontradictory*, the whole package of directives should mimic the way the individual directives display the relationships of *temporality, action-orientation, practicality, and fittingness*. For instance, the temporal ordering of the stated directives must make sense in terms of what is to occur in any necessary time-sequence. The combination of actions must make sense in terms of facilitating rather than complicating or obfuscating what is to be enacted. The combined set of directives must coalesce in such a way that its doability and appropriateness is meaningfully expressed in the language used.

In summary, I conclude that a grammar of curriculum practice, having structured relationships among its key components and activities, should be conceptualized as follows:

A *grammar of curriculum practice is stipulated to consist of:* (1) *the specification of the constituent component concepts inherent in the phenomenon of curriculum;* (2) *the specification of the constituent operational concepts inherent in curriculum practice;* (3) *the specification of the relationships and interrelationships between these two sets of concepts as they are structured by the principles of consistency, noncontradiction, temporality, action-orientation, coherence, practicality, and fittingness; and* (4) *their meaningful formulation and communication in the design of a complete and unified curriculum prescribed for a particular educational setting and circumstance.*

This definition of a grammar of curriculum practice embraces all the elements of what is to be said and done in curriculum planning, all the elements that define a curriculum, and all the criteria for relating these elements in meaningful and actionable ways as curriculum practitioners decide what to prescribe in a curriculum plan.

Notice that this definition exhibits a definite structure of concepts and processes necessary for conducting curriculum practice. It posits a singular conceptualization that requires no further speculation about the task to be undertaken, the steps to be followed, the concepts and actions to be employed, or the form and types of prescriptions to be made in formulating a curriculum plan. It is singularly a grammar of curriculum practice.

Table 4.1 summarizes this conceptualization of a grammar of curriculum practice by graphically representing all of its elements and identifying each of its constituent concepts and their relationship to one another. These constitutive concepts were defined at various points earlier in this book, and their definitions are restated in box 4.1, where they are listed in one place for convenient reference when viewing table 4.1 and to assist in recognizing their place in this entire conceptualization of a grammar of curriculum practice. The additional feature to be noted in the right-hand column of table 4.1 is the identification of the semantic relationships among these concepts, as characterized earlier in this section.

This conceptualization of a grammar of curriculum practice, composed of these stipulated key concepts and their stated relationships, is conceived as a way of clarifying and making intelligible the work of curriculum practice so that curriculum practitioners have a common basis for understanding and carrying out what is to be said and done in their work. This conception of a grammar of curriculum practice can serve as a basis for what is to occur in curriculum practice.[2]

Table 4.1. A Grammar of Curriculum Practice: Its Constituent Concepts and Semantic Structure

Categories	Constituent Concepts	Semantic Relationships for Each Concept
The Task of Curriculum Practice	To prescribe a complete curriculum plan (e.g., Pre-K–12)	Coherence
The Field of Prescriptions to Be Addressed	All ten components of curriculum (table 2.4)	Consistent and non-contradictory across components
The Specific Topics to Be Prescribed	Multiple topics within each of the ten components of curriculum and across all components	Consistent and noncontradictory across topics
The Process for Determining Preferences for Every Specific Topic Prescribed	Deliberation (identify options, state reasons for desirability, assess arguments for and against, choose options with strongest arguments for, reach consensus on best option)	Temporality, action-orientation, practicality, fittingness
The Ways Chosen Preferences Are to Be Conceived	As prescribed conceptions and actions	Temporality, action-orientation, practicality, fittingness

The Way Each Prescribed Conception and Action Is to Be Formulated	As a directive with both an ideational component and an action verb (except with assumptive component state doctrines and rationale and with contextual realities component assert facts and explanation)	Consistency, noncontradictory, temporality, action-orientation practicality, fittingness
The Way the Entire Set of Directives Is to Be Structured and Interrelated	As a prescribed complete curriculum action plan composed of all directives combined in a unified and integral whole	Coherence, consistency, noncontradictory, temporality, action-orientation, practicality, fittingness

Box 4.1
Collected Definitions of Constituent Concepts in a Grammar of Curriculum Practice
(all previously given earlier in this book)

The first set of concepts that form a part of a grammar of curriculum practice consists of those that define the constituent components of the phenomenon of curriculum (see table 2.4 for the list of the definitions of these ten components).

The second set of concepts that form a part of a grammar of curriculum practice consists of those that constitute the work of curriculum practice, which in its overall conceptualization was defined as follows:

> *Curriculum practice is stipulated to be a series of deliberations on the preferred conceptions and actions to be prescribed in a particular curriculum plan (addressing all ten components of a complete curriculum) and the formulation of the resulting preferences in clearly specified directives for the conceptions and actions that are to be enacted.*

The three constitutive operational concepts inherent in this definition were identified as *deliberation*, *preferred conceptions and actions*, and *prescriptions formulated as directives*, each of which was further defined below.

> *Deliberation is stipulated to consist of five actions required to reach a decision on any aspect of curriculum work, each of which is construed as follows:*
>
> 1. *identify substantive options/alternatives/choices to be considered;*
> 2. *state reasons why each option is or is not a desirable one;*

> 3. assess strengths and weaknesses of the arguments across options;
> 4. identify the options for which the strongest arguments can be made; and
> 5. reach consensus on which option is the best, all things considered.

> Conceptions and actions are stipulated to be the only appropriate types of outcomes of curriculum deliberation where conceptions are construed as ideational features and actions are construed as direct imperatives to act.

> Directives are stipulated to be the most appropriate kind of statement in which to formulate the prescribed conceptions and actions resulting from curriculum deliberations in all components of a curriculum except for the assumptive and the contextual realities components where, respectively, doctrines and factual statements are most appropriate.

> A directive is construed as a statement containing both a precise explanation of a particular prescribed conception or action that is to be implemented and a narrowly focused action verb(s) specifying what is to be said or done to implement that conception or action.

While assumptions and contextual realities cannot be prescribed in the form of directives, they can be formulated as doctrines or as factual statements, each defined as follows:

> A doctrine is construed as a statement containing an explicit assertion of, and arguments for, a particular belief or value (or set of beliefs or values) that is (are) intended to undergird some other selected curriculum decision(s); and

> *a factual statement is construed as a statement containing an explicit description of the prevailing state of affairs in some domain of contextual reality along with persuasive evidence of its empirical validity for use as a basis for making some other selected curriculum decision(s).*

Chapter 5

The Value and Use of a Grammar of Curriculum Practice

Some reflections on this conceptualization of a grammar of curriculum practice may contribute to an understanding of its value and use.

The first observation is that this grammar of curriculum practice embraces quite well the notion that curriculum work is a *practice*, as it was defined in chapter 1, where I adopted the following definition:

> A *practice is a series of sayings and doings undertaken by a person or persons to accomplish an intended purpose in a given domain of socially valued activity.*

This is a simplified version of a definition that was quoted from a scholarly study of practice: "[A practice is] *a socially established cooperative human activity involving utterances and forms of understanding (sayings), modes of action (doings), and ways in which people relate to one another and the world (relatings) that 'hang together' in characteristic ways in a distinctive 'project'* " (Mahon et al., 2017).

Both of these statements place what is said and done at the center of conducting a practice, which is the perspective taken by this grammar of curriculum practice. The point of view inherent in this idea is that of the persons doing the work of curriculum, not of someone describing it or otherwise analyzing or dealing with it from an external point of view. It is an existential perspective and is embodied in the language and action of those who themselves are engaged in the practice. The concepts and processes defined and explained in this grammar of curriculum practice are ones that can be used by curriculum practitioners with a minimum of uncertainty about what is to be done and how to do it, as they engage in producing a curriculum.

In constructing this grammar of curriculum practice, it should also be noted, it has been necessary to confront and attempt to resolve two long-standing problems faced in curriculum work, to wit, how best to conceive of the phenomenon of curriculum and how best to conceive of the phenomenon of curriculum work. An attempt has been made to address both of these problems and to defend the conceptions put forth. While it remains to be seen whether adopting and using these conceptions (the ten components of curriculum and the deliberating on and prescribing of directives related to these components) will facilitate the direction and progress of the work of curriculum practitioners, this grammar has identified and elucidated a new and creative way of thinking about such matters intended to overcome some of the limitations of conventional language and practices employed in the past in this field of work. These new conceptions of curriculum and of how curriculum decisions should be made can be utilized at all levels of curriculum decision making whether local, state, or national.

In addition to clarifying the nature of curriculum and of curriculum practice, the development, definition, and adoption of several new concepts in place of certain conventional concepts used in the past were involved in constructing this grammar of curriculum practice. Such terms as *curriculum development*, *change processes* or *strategies*, *solving curriculum problems*, *design steps*, and *decision-making* have been abandoned for being too general, too imprecise, or not accurately representing the realities of curriculum work as it needs to be perceived by those who have to engage in it. In their place I have introduced the concepts of deliberation, the promulgation of directives, and the coherent bundling of them in clear ideas and action verbs to form a meaningful and operationally viable curriculum plan for enactment. These concepts have been given detailed definitions to bring clarity and precise meaning to their use in curriculum discourses and activities. The language of curriculum practice is thereby made more functional and focused than that used in times past.

This grammar also provides a singular conceptualization of all these matters—one that is more likely to be acceptable to participants in curriculum work than many offered in the past. Because of the extensive and rather exhaustive supporting arguments presented in its favor, they may be able to agree to adopt this approach to curriculum work. This is an advantage in a circumstance where it is common to find individuals participating in curriculum work holding somewhat different conceptions of the task before them (and of what constitutes a curriculum), thus causing no end of difficulty in arriving at decisions (in addition to those difficulties arising from differences about what should be preferred among substantive options). It has often been the case that much time and energy is spent by curriculum workers trying to adjudicate differences in their conceptions of their task and of the procedures to be followed before they are able to proceed with making actual curriculum decisions. This grammar offers a way out of this dilemma by stipulating an approach all participants can agree to adopt.

It is hoped that these new concepts that comprise this grammar of curriculum practice will allow curriculum practitioners to engage in their work with more conceptually adequate tools than were available to them in the past and will enable them to accomplish their work with more assurance that it will be enacted as desired in real educational settings with actual students and teachers.

Another matter worth observing about this grammar of curriculum practice is that it is value-free—in the sense that it can be utilized with any number of curriculum visions and perspectives that curriculum practitioners may hold or wish to assert as good and desirable. It does not require any particular way of viewing the purposes of curriculum or any particular way of conceiving curriculum content or subject matter; it does not require any particular way of organizing the curriculum or of understanding teaching or learning; it does not require any particular way of organizing or writing up a curriculum plan. It is entirely open at every point to any and all possible ways of conceiving and handling these matters. The only requirements dictated by this grammar of curriculum practice are that its activities be built around the ten curriculum components in the form of associated directives and that it uses appropriate concepts and language necessary to present these desired prescriptions as clearly and usefully as possible.

It should be noted that this book has taken the stance that the phenomenon of curriculum should be conceptualized as separate and distinct from the phenomena of teaching and/or instruction. This view was taken because of the tendency in conventional practice to conflate the two phenomena and use such concepts as aims and objectives, content, methods, and evaluation in both domains without acknowledging that their referents could not be the same when discussing larger, overall curriculum decisions and when discussing narrower, teaching or instructional decisions. The confusion arising from this use of terminology has plagued both the practice of curriculum and the practice of teaching for decades and has hindered the effective conduct of both. Much of the conventional language and practice that has centered on these ambiguous terms is, no doubt, better suited to the domain of teaching and learning where specificity is desired and warranted. This book has attempted to identify and label distinctly different concepts as these topics apply to broad curricular decisions (e.g., purposes, unique long-term objectives, general substantive subject matter, and evaluation of plans rather than of learning).

Notwithstanding the effort to clearly distinguish curriculum from teaching conceptually in this book, it must be acknowledged that an intimate connection does indeed exist between the two in practice. A curriculum plan lays out what and how teaching and learning are to be conceived and enacted. The conduct of teaching and of learning without having a clear view of what is to be focused on and how it should be addressed both conceptually and in action is to have to rely on the immediate judgment of teachers and other actors in a given educational situation without benefit of boarder, more deliberative understandings of what is at stake from the point of view of both the students and the society in which they are being educated. Curriculum decisions made through the deliberative process are essentially decisions about what is best in a given circumstance, all things considered, not just what might be considered best at the time of teaching and learning by those who happen to be involved.

Also apparent in this conceptualization of a grammar of curriculum practice is the fact that it eschews the adding of any specialized program or trendy topic to a curriculum without reference to whether it is consistent with its overall purposes and directives. Quite often special curricula, such as, for instance, ethnic studies or antibullying programs, are added to an already existing curriculum with no attempt to integrate these additional initiatives into its underlying design and structure. In fact, the temptation is to keep adding various pieces or projects until there is no longer clear evidence of an overall design that makes up the entire curriculum, thus making its enactment increasingly difficult and confusing. This grammar views curriculum work as requiring the production of a unified, integral curriculum plan that incorporates everything that is intended to be included in it without leaving any unintegrated or inconsistent pieces appended to it that have not been fully deliberated about and articulated into the total plan. This approach facilitates the work of enacting the curriculum by avoiding competing or contradictory directives that may result from disparate programs or curricular elements existing alongside the planned curriculum.

Curriculum practitioners who choose to follow this grammar of curriculum practice should find their role in the whole array of decision-making surrounding curriculum policy-making, program planning, and student experiences much less uncertain than has been the case in the past. The problem of who should make which decisions across this whole range of curricular and instructional decisions has been unresolved for far too long, despite valiant attempts to assign roles and functions at various levels (see Myers, 1970; Marsh and Willis, 2007), which in reality are never quite adhered to in actual practice. This grammar clearly stipulates what decisions are curricular decisions (the ten components) but recognizes that what distinguishes the choices made for these components at the policy level, the planning level, or the enactment level is the degree of specificity of the directives prescribed: very broad and open-ended at the policy level; very particular, practical, and actionable at the program-planning level; and closely tailored to the students and their particular learning circumstances at the enactment level. Curriculum practitioners are concerned only with the middle-level decisions in this continuum. They take the broad policy outlines provided to them by their parent agency and flesh out a plan of action that embodies those policies in practical terms. And they leave the matter of interpreting and enacting their plan to teachers who work with students in actual educational settings. As curriculum practitioners, they have specific tasks and processes to follow in conducting their practice (deliberation and the production of directives for the entire curriculum plan).

The way this grammar of curriculum practice defines and structures curriculum work assumes that curriculum practitioners will be afforded sufficient freedom to conduct their practice in the manner that is stipulated in this conceptualization of curriculum practice. If the parent agency under which they work unwisely presents them with overly prescriptive mandates or dictates very specific elements to be included in a curriculum plan, the deliberations by curriculum practitioners will become more restricted, and other options, however suitable they might judge them to be for the circumstances they are addressing, could be excluded from consideration. On the other hand, if the directives given by a parent agency are insufficiently spelled out and do not provide enough clarity regarding intended purposes, assumptions, or other matters on which to base an acceptable curriculum plan, curriculum practitioners may feel free to fill in specifications that enable them to create a total, internally consistent curriculum plan despite the absence of such statements. If, however, they receive directives that they consider incompatible with one another and that cannot be coherently embedded in a plan, they should probably seek revisions in the directives from the parent agency. The freedom of curriculum practitioners to set directives within their prescribed curriculum plan is certainly not total or arbitrary, since they must work within what they are given and allow sufficient freedom to those who will enact the plan to interpret their directives in ways that fit varying teaching and learning situations as they arise over time with various students.

Curriculum practitioners who follow this grammar may wonder where to begin in constructing their curriculum plans. It was earlier suggested that there is no particular order required in deliberating their decisions on the ten components of curriculum. Undoubtedly, there will be a good deal of going back and forth from one of these components to another as they attempt to make their directives consistent with one another throughout their plan. Nevertheless, the initial task may well be to grasp an explicit vision of what the curriculum is intended to accomplish as it is to be planned and enacted—its purposes and unique objectives—so that the rest of the decisions they make will line up with this vision. If policy statements are sufficiently clear on these matters, this initial task may be relatively easy to explicate. If not, some effort must be made to articulate the nature of this vision, its purposes, and its unique objectives before moving on to other decisions. There are numerous resources available in the literature of curriculum to which one may turn for assistance if such a vision is not readily discernible from the policy statements provided. Finding and sorting out appropriate examples in the literature is not easy, but a starting point may be to consult formal curriculum proposals that have been collected and summarized (see Short, 2020; 2021).

This grammar has implications for many changes from current practices in several related realms such as the preparation of curriculum practitioners, arrangements for organizing and supporting the work of curriculum practitioners, the work of teachers and other educators who must enact the prescribed plans of curriculum practitioners, and the organization and communication of curriculum scholarship and research related to curriculum practice—all of which need to be worked out by people working in these other realms of practice.[1]

Having completed a series of reflections on the value and use of this conceptualization of a grammar of curriculum practice, a brief summary is provided in box 5.1 by way of highlighting its advantages over other more traditional conceptualizations.

Box 5.1
Highlights of this Conceptualization of a Grammar of Curriculum Practice

1. It conceives curriculum work to be a deliberative professional practice with an explicit but limited function and well-defined tasks to accomplish, thus overcoming the vagueness of earlier conceptualizations of curriculum work.
2. It conceives curriculum work from the perspective of those actually engaged in doing curriculum work rather than from the perspective of an external analyst who studies or theorizes about it, thus reflecting the existential experience of those who must in situ decide what to say and do in order to carry out their work.
3. It establishes the essential components that constitute a curriculum and the essential tasks that constitute curriculum practice, thus solving two long-standing dilemmas faced by curriculum workers—having to choose among multiple competing conceptions of curriculum and of curriculum practice, where no conclusive argument

favoring any of the available options is apparent—and thus making it easier to accept these concepts as being constituent components rather than merely recommended or arbitrary ones.
4. It conceives of curriculum in sufficiently generic and value-free terms, so that it can embrace any and all visions of a preferred curriculum, thus meeting the criticism that some earlier conceptualizations of curriculum were too narrow or so ideologically biased that certain visions of curriculum were conceptually incompatible with their terminology.
5. It identifies distinctive new concepts that are uniquely useful in thinking about curriculum and doing curriculum work separate from those useful in thinking about and doing the work of teaching, thus overcoming the frequent conflation and use of the same terms in both of these domains.
6. It argues that any curriculum plan created by utilizing the concepts and tasks set forth in this conceptualization must be internally consistent and coherent, thus eschewing the tendency to add programs or trendy topics without fully integrating them into the plan or recognizing them as being incompatible or inconsistent with the intent and structure of the entire plan and, therefore, making it necessary that they be excluded.
7. It identifies the precise role and scope of curriculum work within the curriculum policy-making/program planning/teacher-student transactions continuum of decision-making, thus clarifying the often contested and/or overlapping jurisdictions of those working at these various levels.
8. It assumes that curriculum work will be afforded sufficient freedom to set preferred curriculum directives within the broad preferences set by parent agencies, and yet be constrained from overprescribing what those who will need

sufficient latitude in enacting their plans must determine at their level, thus being recognized as an independent but responsible professional practice.
9. It does not prescribe a precise order or sequence of decisions that curriculum workers shall follow in producing a curriculum plan, only that all curriculum components be addressed while keeping all decisions consistent with the intended purposes and unique objectives as stated, and adhering to criteria for obtaining meaningful relationships among all parts of the plan, thus preserving the necessary flexibility to revisit all decisions until unity and coherence is obtained throughout the entire plan.
10. It has a number of features that reflect a departure from prevailing practice, such that work in related realms will need to be addressed differently as well (e.g., the preparation of curriculum practitioners, arrangements for organizing and supporting this work, orienting teachers and others who will enact their plans, useful related research, etc.), thus implying that successful utilization of this grammar of curriculum practice depends on work done in these other realms as well as that done by curriculum practitioners themselves.

Chapter 6

What This Book Has Attempted to Do

The construction of this grammar of curriculum practice has been a scholarly activity—primarily an analytic and conceptual endeavor. It has not been one of substantive curriculum criticism, nor has it been one of constructing or justifying educational doctrines, proposals, or reforms. It has not been one of describing or mapping the work of curriculum practice, nor of locating this work in its intellectual/social/historical context. It has not been one of linking the expertise associated with curriculum practice with the expertise it draws on from outside its practice, nor of establishing correct or incorrect understandings of curriculum practice. It has been a practical endeavor arising out of the necessities and contingencies of curriculum practice and a desire to improve how it is carried on and to improve the concepts and activities it employs in its essential discourses and practices. This grammar of curriculum practice has intended to be useful to curriculum practitioners and to those who must understand and support what they do.

It is my observation that over the last several decades curriculum work has suffered from neglect, both in the world of educational practice and in the scholarly world of curriculum studies. The emphasis in educational settings has been on teaching, teaching methods, learning objectives, content standards, student assessment, and accountability, while leaving policy-makers, educational leaders, teachers, and the public believing that curriculum work has already been addressed by others (most especially by specifying content standards and accountability practices). This book clearly reminds us that these trends have left virtually unaddressed the real work of curriculum planning. So-called content standards (as usually conceived) do not constitute a curriculum. Learning objectives (as usually conceived for the classroom) do not typically embrace long-range curriculum purposes or visions of the educated person. Evaluation practices notoriously focus on narrow features of teaching and learning rather than on the broader features of curriculum and its multiple components. Better conceptualizations of what constitutes curriculum and curriculum work have been absent and much needed. Neglect by our scholars of an examination and critique of those practices has been accompanied by a similar neglect of developing a fully articulated conceptualization of curriculum and of curriculum work as well.

The point of my making these observations on the contemporary educational scene is that the intellectual tools provided by a viable grammar of curriculum practice can be a part of what is needed to confront the notion that curriculum issues are settled, or sufficiently settled, so that the only important questions to be resolved are those concerning how teaching and learning should proceed. This grammar can help refocus attention on the neglected work of curriculum practice and provide helpful assistance in conceptualizing and conducting curriculum work and in defining what curriculum itself actually involves. It is my hope that this book is a step in the direction of constructing a grammar of curriculum practice that will provide the necessary intellectual tools for more adequately conceiving and conducting curriculum work in the future.[1]

This book is a creative work aimed at producing a representation of a grammar of curriculum practice that enables clear and effective use of language in settings where curriculum practice is undertaken. It addresses the enactment of curriculum discourses and practices by curriculum practitioners. It undertakes systematic reflection on the distinctive words and discourses and the distinctive deeds and practices employed by curriculum practitioners. Its aim is to formulate an outline or grammar of curriculum discourse and practice, not to make preferred prescriptions for curriculum discourse and practice. Thus, the emphasis is on analyzing and clarifying the language of curriculum discourse and curriculum practice and on identifying structures that underlie the variety of terminology and language that surface in ordinary curriculum discourse and practice. This grammar constitutes the fundamental structure of knowledge of curriculum discourses and practices on which particular formulations of curriculum discourses, doctrines, actions, and practices can be expressed and utilized.[2]

Closing Summary

In summary, this book has argued that curriculum work should be understood to be a professional practice, the purpose of which is to outline a plan for a curriculum by means of deliberating the preferred conceptions and actions for the ten constituent components of curriculum and by communicating these preferences in the form of prescriptive statements (either assertions for thought and action or of factual realities or of doctrinal beliefs) expressed as practical, readily actionable directives for implementation by those who will enact the prescribed plan.

Notes

Introduction

1. This book primarily uses the intellectual tools of philosophical and conceptual analysis to address the topic of a grammar of curriculum practice. That is, this endeavor involves the analysis, development, critique, synthesis, and organization of concepts in the process of discerning, clarifying, and constructing the essential nature of curriculum practice. It is concerned with analyzing and critiquing concepts traditionally employed in this practice when deemed inadequately conceived, imprecise, or incoherently related in a viable conceptual structure. It is also a creative task concerned with concept development and replacement when more adequately conceived, more precise, or more structurally coherent concepts would appear to be justified. I draw on sources from philosophical and conceptual analysis such as Daniels (1971), Steiner (1978), Daniels and Coombs (1982), Coombs and Daniels (1991), and Grove and Short (1991). The title of this book is meant to suggest that it is an initial attempt to produce a grammar of curriculum practice and that it should be examined, elucidated, critiqued, and enhanced by others before being considered an adequate representation of a grammar of curriculum practice.

Chapter 1

1. Here and elsewhere in this book I have chosen to present the results of various analyses I have done without giving detailed

explanations of how I reached those conclusions. This approach should enable readers to keep focused on the central arguments of the text without having to follow the intricacies of every analysis I have done. Those who wish to check the accuracy of any of the conclusions I have drawn from these analyses should, of course, proceed to analyze the topics for themselves. It is also important to note that the purpose of doing these analyses here and on other topics later in this book is to be able to define with as much precision as possible the key terms I have adopted. This requires clearly distinguishing what is incorporated within the definition and what is not. In arriving at definitions, I have followed guidelines offered by analytic philosophers such as Ayer (1946, chapter 3), Alston (1964), Hospers (1967), Robinson (1972), Gorovitz (1979), and Gupta (2019).

Chapter 2

1. For historical reviews of the concept of curriculum, see Hamilton (1989, 1990), Jackson (1992), Doll (2002), and Jonnaert and Thevriault (2013). A compilation of fifty-six definitions of curriculum published before 1970 can be found in Weldon (1970). For historical reviews of curriculum making, see Bostwick (1957); Cremin (1971); Clegg (1976); and Craig and Ross (2008).

2. Examples of using the tools of conceptual analysis to examine the domain of curriculum and its components are to be found in the following sources by curriculum scholars who have had extensive experience with curriculum practice: Faix (1964), Macagnoni (1970), Goodlad (1979, coda), Beauchamp (1981), and Jonnaert and Thevriault (2013) analyze whole systems of concepts related to curriculum; Macdonald (1965), Lamm (1969), Johnson (1977), Laska (1984), Huebner (1991), Thijs and van den Akker (2009), and Gordon, Taylor, and Oliva (2019) analyze the domain of instruction in relation to the domain of curriculum; Smith (1963), Boomer (1992), and Deng (2017) analyze the distinction between teaching and curriculum.

3. Although the components listed in table 2.3 related to learning, teaching, and instruction are excluded from curriculum, scholars and practitioners involved in these other domains will find the conceptual work done on those topics by the authors cited in that table worthy of their consideration. Curriculum scholars often present insights from

their perspectives that do not occur to those working in these other domains. Also several sources concerned with translating curriculum into teaching and instructional plans are worthy of study and application: Johnson (1969), Schwab (1973), Harris (1985), and Hyun (2006).

4. I have offered a redefinition of curriculum and have asserted that it be the framework on which a total curriculum practice should be built (in order to be both theoretically sound and practically viable). But, this effort is tentative and is subject to future analysis and development. As Bill Green says, "There is much to be done to deepen and extend our understanding of what it is to speak of curriculum; to seek to realize curriculum, to reflect on its nature and meaning; its value, and its effect; and to nurture a fully developed curriculum imagination" (2018, 14).

Chapter 3

1. Not included in this listing of empirical studies of curriculum practice (planning/development) are studies of such related but different realms of practice as organization and administration of curriculum policy-making, the organization and support of personnel doing curriculum planning, the managing of curriculum development/implementation/revision, the development of curriculum materials, the conduct of actual enactment of curriculum via teaching and learning, and so on, such as those found in Schaffarzick (1975); McClure (1979); Young (1979); Kennedy (1990); Marsh et al. (1990); Torres (1999); Rosenmund et al. (2002); Mfum-Mensah (2009); Molsad (2015); McPhail (2016); Priestley and Philipou (2018). Also excluded are textbook treatments of these administrative activities that necessarily support and implement curriculum practice (e.g., Glatthorn et al., 2018). Neither of these kinds of sources can provide evidence of what uniquely goes on within the domain of curriculum practice itself. Consequently, such sources are not among those cited in this chapter on how curriculum work has been conceptualized.

2. For a view of deliberation as first developed by Aristotle, see McKeon (1952) and Englund (2006). Expanded treatments of deliberation and its role in curriculum practice can be found in Knitter (1985), Roby (1985); Harris (1986, 1991); Dillon (1994), McCutcheon (1995); Reid (1999), and Walker (2003, ch. 7).

3. Case studies of what actually occurs in situations where curriculum deliberation is employed can provide additional insights on how deliberation functions operationally. They, however, do not usually offer explicit definitions of deliberation, and so I have not been able to include any definitions from case studies in the listing in box 3.4. See, for example, Walker (1975); Wise (1979); Orpwood (1985); Bonser and Grundy (1988); Kennedy (1988, 1990); Mulder (1991, 1994); Holt (1990, 1994); McCutcheon (1995); Shkedi (1996); and Lam (2011).

Chapter 4

1. Some readers might have thought that this book should be called "a logic of curriculum practice" rather than "a grammar of curriculum practice." But this endeavor does not require the establishing of theorems or postulates that follow the rules of logic, deduction, or induction (although these processes certainly can be employed at various points in the process of conducting curriculum practice—especially concerning decisions on curricular assumptions and contextual realities that are based on particular doctrines or facts). Rather, the construction of a grammar of curriculum practice requires that we exhibit a way in which the particular concepts constituting curriculum and curriculum practice can be related and interrelated so that intelligible and meaningful communication and action can be undertaken in conducting curriculum work. This process in not governed by rules, as in the case of logic. It is essentially an artistic task in which elements are placed in relation to each other to make an integral whole (see Schatzki, 1996, ch. 4).

2. I concede that it would be desirable to include in this book an example of a complete curriculum plan that has followed the process outlined in this conceptualization of a grammar of curriculum practice. I cannot present such an example, however, since no one has yet put one together using this approach, and I have chosen not to create a hypothetical one to present as an illustration. We shall have to wait to offer such an example until some group of curriculum practitioners prescribes a particular curriculum plan using this conceptualization of a grammar of curriculum practice. I should also concede that this conceptualization, though its appropriateness for use is strongly argued for in this book, is probably not the only formulation of a grammar of

curriculum practice that is possible. If this one does not seem suitable in the view of other curriculum practitioners or scholars, they should attempt to construct a more viable one.

Chapter 5

1. Implications of this grammar of curriculum practice for related realms of practice might include the following:

   1. *For the education and training of curriculum practitioners:* the study of curriculum (conceived as consisting of its ten components), the study of curriculum work as a practice (consisting of doing deliberations and the formulation of curriculum plans), participation as apprentices in ongoing curriculum work with active curriculum practitioners, and in-service experiences in a variety of different settings where curriculum prescriptions of various kinds are being deliberated and plans developed.

   2. *For the administrative support for curriculum practice:* assessing when new curriculum work is required by changing circumstances, determining criteria for and appointment of those who are to be tasked with doing the work of curriculum practice; activating and monitoring this work, and arranging time, facilities, and funding for this work and for in-service education of those involved.

   3. *For teaching and learning practices:* discovering how and when the directives in a prescribed curriculum may require particular nontraditional (or traditional) ways of teaching or of arranging student learning environments; discovering how they may affect course, unit, or lesson planning in new ways; how student assessment of learning may need to differ from past practices; and how to keep the vision and long-range purposes of the prescribed curriculum constantly in view during planning, teaching, and the activities of student learning.

4. *For the work of curriculum scholars and researchers:* doing studies of actual curriculum practice (especially the examination of the sayings and doings that occur in such work), and identifying and organizing the myriad substantive options that already exist (or have been proposed) for each of the ten curriculum components. Especially helpful would be identifying and collating the subject matter options that are so vast and complex and so difficult for curriculum practitioners to keep abreast of (e.g., changes in the realms of knowledge, skills, dispositions, ways of being, etc.). Conventional topics and methods of scholarly inquiry are by no means ruled out by these new research tasks; they need only to be supplemented by approaches such as those mentioned that can meet the immediate needs of curriculum practitioners for useful and competent intellectual resources.

Chapter 6

1. This book focuses on the intricate derivation and defense of a set of concepts making up a viable grammar of curriculum practice; what must follow this work is the articulation of specific guidelines for engaging in actual curriculum practice based on this conceptualization. These might take the form of an instructional manual, an agenda for training workshops, an outline for an academic course and practicum, or practical activities for coaching or consulting with Pre-K–12 curriculum practitioners actively involved in doing curriculum work. Anyone interested in developing such resources and/or taking leadership in adopting the concepts set forth in this grammar of curriculum practice as a practical basis for curriculum planning, is invited to do so and to be in touch with the author of this book.

2. In constructing this grammar of curriculum practice, certain key concepts generated by leading scholars have struck me as particularly salient in moving the discourse and practice of curriculum forward in desired directions. I wish to identify some of these ideas and their authors and to acknowledge with gratitude their seminal contributions to this book. They include: *practice as activity-driven not theory-derived*

(Bourdieu, 1977; Polkinghorne, 2004); *curriculum as a practice* (Schwab, 1969; Stenhouse, 1975; Walker, 1971, 1992, 2003; Goodlad, 1979; Deng, 2018); *curriculum components* (Posner, 1992/2004; van den Akker, 2003); *curriculum as a moral enterprise* (Huebner, 1966; Macdonald, 1977, 1986; Reid, 1978, 1999); *curriculum deliberation* (Schwab, 1969); *the analysis and development of concepts* (Soltis, 1968; Coombs & Daniels, 1991); *synthesis of scholarly work requires analysis and concept creation* (Hurd, 1983; Strike & Posner, 1983); and *grammar of discourses and practices* (Jones, 2002; Schatzki, 2012).

References

Alston, W. P. (1964). *Philosophy of language*. Prentice-Hall.
Argyris, C., & Schon, D. A. (1974). *Theory in practice: Increasing professional effectiveness*. Jossey-Bass.
Austin, J. L. (1975). *How to do things with words* (2nd ed.). Harvard University Press.
Ayer, A. J. (1946). *Language, truth and logic* (2nd ed.). Dover.
Beauchamp, G. A. (1961). *Curriculum theory*. Kagg Press.
Beauchamp, G. A. (1981). *Curriculum theory* (4th ed.). F. E. Peacock.
Ben-Peretz, M., & Tamir, P. (1986). What do curricular developers do? *Curriculum Perspectives*, 6(2), 8–15.
Berman, L. M., Hultgren, F. L., Lee, D., Rivkin, M. S., & Roderick, J. A. (1991). *Toward curriculum for being*. State University of New York Press.
Bertalanffy, L. (1968). *General system theory: Foundations, development, applications*. G. G. Braziller.
Biesta, G. J. (2013). Knowledge, judgment and the curriculum: On the past, present and future of the idea of the practical. *Journal of Curriculum Studies*, 45(5), 684–696.
Biesta, G. J., & Stengel, B. S. (2016). Thinking philosophically about teaching. In D. H. Gitomer & C. A. Bell (Eds.), *Handbook of research on teaching* (5th ed.) (pp. 7–67). American Educational Research Association.
Billett, S., Harteis, C., & Gruber, H. (Eds.). (2014). *International handbook of research in professional and practice-based learning*. Springer.
Bobbitt, F. (1924). *How to make a curriculum*. Houghton Mifflin.
Boersma, K., & Looy, F. (1997). *Een praktijktheorie voor leerplanontwikkeling [A practice theory for curriculum development]*. Netherlands Institute for Curriculum Development.

Bonser, S. A., & Grundy, S. J. (1988). Reflective deliberation in the formulation of a school curriculum policy. *Journal of Curriculum Studies, 20*(1), 35–45.

Boomer, G. (1992). Curriculum composing and evaluating. In G. Boomer, N. Lester, C. Onore, & J. Cook (Eds.), *Negotiating the curriculum: Educating for the 21st century* (pp. 32–45). Falmer Press.

Bostwick, P., Parker, J. C., & Potter, G. L. (1957). *One hundred years of curriculum improvement, 1857–1957*. Association for Supervision and Curriculum Development.

Bourdieu, P. (1977). *Outline of a theory of practice*. Cambridge University Press.

Broudy, H. S., Smith, B. O., & Burnett, J. R. (1966). *Democracy and excellence in American secondary education*. Rand McNally.

Carr, D. (2014). Professionalism, profession and professional conduct: Towards a basic logical and ethical geography. In S. Billett, C. Harteis, & H. Gruber (Eds.), *International handbook of research in professional and practice-based learning* (pp. 5–27). Springer.

Chen, D., Wang, L., & Neo, W. (2015). School-based curriculum development towards a culture of learning: Nonlinearity in practice. *British Journal of Educational Studies, 63*(2), 213–228.

Christensen, J. E., & Fisher, J. E. (1979). *Analytic philosophy of education as a subdiscipline of educology*. University Press of America.

Clandinin, D. J. (1985). Personal practical knowledge: A study of teacher's classroom images, *Curriculum Inquiry, 15*(4), 361–385.

Clegg, A. A., Jr. (1976). Diversity and conformity in American curriculum. In O. L. Davis Jr. (Ed.), *Perspectives on curriculum development: 1776–1976* (pp. 175–213). Association for Supervision and Curriculum Development.

Connelly, F. M. (1974). Research problems in curriculum: Alternative paradigms. ERIC Document Reproduction Service. ED 091 814.

Connelly, F. M., & Clandinin, D. J. (1985). Personal practical knowledge and the modes of knowing: Relevance for teaching and learning. In E. W. Eisner (Ed.), *Learning and teaching the ways of knowing* (pp. 174–198). University of Chicago Press.

Connelly, F. M., & Clandinin, D. J. (1988). *Teachers as curriculum planners: Narratives of experience*. Teachers College Press.

Connelly, F. M., He, M. F., & Phillion, J. (Eds.) (2008). Planning the handbook: Practice, context, and theory. In *The Sage handbook of curriculum and instruction* (pp. ix–xv). Sage Publications.

Connelly, F. M., & Xu, S. (2010). An overview of research in curriculum inquiry. In P. Peterson, E. Baker, & B. McGaw (Eds.), *International encyclopedia of education* (3rd ed.) (pp. 324–334). Elsevier.

Connelly, F. M., & Xu, S. (2012). Curriculum and curriculum studies. In J. Arthur & A. Peterson (Eds.), *The Routledge companion to education* (pp. 115–124). Routledge.

Coombs, J. R., & Daniels, L. B. (1991). Philosophical inquiry: Conceptual analysis. In E. C. Short (Ed.), *Forms of curriculum inquiry* (pp. 27–41). State University of New York Press.

Craig, C. J., & Ross, V. (2008). Cultivating the image of teachers as curriculum makers. In F. M. Connelly, M. F. He, & J. Phillion (Eds.), *The Sage handbook of curriculum and instruction* (pp. 282–305). Sage.

Cremin, L. A. (1971). Curriculum-making in the United States. *Teachers College Record, 73*(2), 207–220. Reprinted in W. F. Pinar (Ed.) (1975), *Curriculum theorizing* (pp. 19–38). McCutchan.

Daniels, L. B. (1971). The justification of curricula. ERIC Document Reproduction Service. ED 050 160.

Daniels, L. B., & Coombs, J. R. (1982). The concept of curriculum. In D. B. Cochrane & M. Schiralli (Eds.), *Philosophy of education: Canadian perspectives* (pp. 251–258). Collier Macmillan Canada.

Danielson, C. (2007). *Enhancing professional practice: A framework for teaching* (2nd ed.). Association for Supervision and Curriculum Development.

Deng, Z. (2017). Rethinking curriculum and teaching. In G. W. Noblet (Ed.), *The Oxford research encyclopedia of education*. DOI:10.1093/acrefore/9780190264093.013.55

Deng, Z. (2018). Contemporary curriculum theorizing: Crisis and resolution, *Journal of Curriculum Studies, 50*(6), 691–710.

Derr, R. L. (1977). Curriculum: A concept elucidation. *Curriculum Inquiry, 7*(2), 145–155.

de Saussure, F. (1986). *Course in general linguistics*. Open Court.

Dillon, J. T. (1994). The questions of deliberation. In J. T. Dillon (Ed.), *Deliberation in education and society* (pp. 3–24). Ablex.

Dillon, J. T. (2009). The questions of curriculum. *Journal of Curriculum Studies, 41*(3), 343–359.

Doll, R. C. (1996). *Curriculum improvement: Decision making and process* (9th ed.). Allyn & Bacon.

Doll, W. E., Jr. (2002). Ghosts and the curriculum. In W. E. Doll Jr., & N. Gough (Eds.), *Curriculum visions* (pp. 23–70). Peter Lang.

Doyle, W. (1986). Content representation in teachers' definitions of academic work. *Journal of Curriculum Studies*, 18(4), 365–379.

Duncan, J. K., & Frymier, J. R. (1967). Explorations in the systematic study of curriculum. *Theory Into Practice*, 6(4), 180–199.

Eash, M. J. (1991). Curriculum components. In A. Lewy (Ed.), *International encyclopedia of curriculum* (pp. 67–69). Pergamon Press.

Egan, Kieran (1978). What is curriculum? *Curriculum Inquiry*, 8(1), 65–72.

Eible, C. V., & Zavarella, J. A. (1979). Curriculum development: A model for action. *NASSP Bulletin*, 63(425), 85–90.

Eisner, E. W. (1979). *The educational imagination: On the design and evaluation of school programs*. Macmillan.

Eisner, E. W. (1998). *The enlightened eye*. Merrill.

Eisner, E. W. (2002). *The educational imagination: On the design and evaluation of school programs* (3rd ed.). Merrill Prentice Hall.

Englund, T. (2015). Toward a deliberative curriculum? *Nordic Journal of Studies in Educational Policy*, 1. DOI: 10.3402/nstep.v1.26558

Eraut, M. (1990). Approaches to curriculum design. In N. Entwistle (Ed.), *Handbook of educational ideas and practices* (pp. 539–553). Routledge.

Faix, T. L. (1964). Toward a science of curriculum: Structural-functional analysis as a conceptual system for curriculum theory and research: A theoretical study [Unpublished doctoral dissertation, University of Wisconsin].

Foshay, A. W. (1987). The curriculum matrix. *The Educational Forum*, 51(4), 341–353.

Frymier, J. (1986). After thirty years of thinking about curriculum. *Theory into Practice*, 25(1), 58–63.

Gagne, R. M., Wager, W. W., Golas, K. C., & Keller, J. M. (2005). *Principles of instructional design* (5th ed.). Wadsworth Thomson.

Gay, G. (1984). Curriculum development. In T. Husen & T. N. Postlethwaite (Eds.), *International encyclopedia of education* (pp. 1170–1179). Pergamon.

Gaztambide-Frenandez, R., & Theissen, D. (2009). There's nothing as theoretical as a good practical. *Curriculum Inquiry*, 39(1), 1–14.

Gitomer, D. H., & Bell, C. A. (Eds.) (2016). *Handbook of research on teaching* (5th ed.). American Educational Research Association.

Glatthorn, A. A. (1987). *Curriculum leadership*. Scott, Foresman.
Glatthorn, A. A., Boschee, F. A., Whitehead, B. M., & Boschee, B. F. (2018). *Curriculum leadership: Strategies for development and implementation* (5th ed.). Sage.
Goodlad, J. I., & associates (1979). *Curriculum inquiry: The study of curriculum practice*. McGraw-Hill.
Gordon, W. R., III, Taylor, R. T., & Oliva, P. F. (2019). *Developing the curriculum: Improving outcomes through systems approaches*. Pearson.
Gorovitz, S. (1979). Definitions. In *Philosophical analysis: An introduction to its language and techniques* (pp. 135–144). Random House.
Green, B. (Ed.) (2009). *Understanding and researching professional practice*. Sense.
Green, B. (2018). Introduction: Engaging curriculum? In *Engaging curriculum: Bridging the curriculum theory and English education divide* (pp. 1–20). Routledge.
Grimmett, P., & Halvorson, M. (2010). From understanding to creating curriculum: The case for the co-evolution of re-conceptualized design with re-conceptualized curriculum. *Curriculum Inquiry, 40*(2), 241–262.
Grove, R. W., & Short, E. C. (1991). Theoretical inquiry: Components and structure. In E. C. Short (Ed.), *Forms of curriculum inquiry* (pp. 211–224). State University of New York Press.
Gupta, A. (2019). Definitions. In E. N. Zalta (Ed.), *The Stanford Encyclopedia of Philosophy*. https://plato.stanford.edu/archives/win2019/entries/definitions/
Hamilton, D. (1989/2018). On the origins of the educational terms class and curriculum. In *Towards a theory of schooling* (pp. 35–55). Falmer/Routledge. Reprinted in B. Baker (Ed.), (2009). *New curriculum history* (pp. 3–20). Sense.
Hamilton, D. (1990). *Curriculum history*. Deakin University.
Harris, I. B. (1983). Forms of discourse and their possibilities for guiding practice: Towards an effective rhetoric. *Journal of Curriculum Studies, 15*(1), 27–42.
Harris, I. B. (1985). An exploration of the role of theories in communication for guiding practitioners. *Journal of Curriculum and Supervision, 1*(1), 27–55.
Harris, I. B. (1986). Communicating the character of 'deliberation.' *Journal of Curriculum Studies, 18*(2), 115–132.

Harris, I. B. (1991). Deliberative inquiry: The arts of planning. In E. C. Short (Ed.), *Forms of curriculum inquiry* (pp. 285–307). State University of New York Press.

Heidegger, M, (1982). *The basic problems of phenomenology*. Indiana University Press.

Herrick, V. E. (1950). The concept of curriculum design. In V. E. Herrick & R. W. Tyler (Eds.), *Toward improved curriculum theory*. University of Chicago Press.

Hlebowitsh, P. S. (2005). *Designing the school curriculum*. Pearson Education.

Holt, M. (1990). Managing curriculum change in a comprehensive school: Conflict, compromise and deliberation. *Journal of Curriculum Studies, 22*(2), 137–148.

Holt, M. (1994). Deliberation in the school. In J. T. Dillon (Ed.), *Deliberation in education and society* (pp. 211–237). Ablex.

Hopkins, L. T. (1929). *Curriculum principles and practices*. B. H. Sanborn.

Hospers, J. (1967). Definition. In *An introduction to philosophical analysis* (2nd ed.) (pp. 18–67). Prentice-Hall.

Huebner, D. E. (1966). Curriculum as a field of study. In H. F. Robinson (Ed.), *Precedents and promise in the curriculum field* (pp. 94–111). Teachers College Press.

Huebner, D. E. (1974). Toward a remaking of curricular language. In W. F. Pinar (Ed.), *Heightened consciousness, cultural revolution, and curriculum theory* (pp. 36–53). McCutchan.

Huebner, D. E. (1975). The tasks of the curriculum theorist. In W. F. Pinar (Ed,), *Curriculum theorizing: The reconceptualists* (pp. 250–270). McCutchan. Reprinted in V. Ellis (Ed.) (1999), *The lure of the transcendent: Collected essays by Dwayne E. Huebner* (pp. 212–230). Lawrence Erlbaum.

Huebner, D. E. (1991). Notes toward a framework for curriculum inquiry. *Journal of Curriculum and Supervision, 6*(2), 145–160.

Huebner, D. E. (1999). The thingness of educational content. In V. Ellis (Ed.) (1999), *The lure of the transcendent: Collected essays by Dwayne E. Huebner* (pp. 198–211). Lawrence Erlbaum.

Hurd, P. (1983). Synthesis processes in curriculum development. In S. A. Ward & L. J. Reed (Eds.), *Knowledge structure and use: Implications for synthesis and interpretation* (pp. 645–670). Temple University Press.

Hyun, E. (2006). Transforming instruction into pedagogy through curriculum negotiation. *Journal of Curriculum and Pedagogy, 3*(1), 136–164.

Iwanska, A. (1979). Praxiology and curriculum. In J. I. Goodlad & associates, *Curriculum inquiry: The study of curriculum practice* (pp. 287–302). McGraw-Hill.

Jackson, P. W. (1980). *The practice of teaching*. Teachers College Press.

Jackson, P. W. (1992). Conceptions of curriculum and curriculum specialists. In P. W. Jackson (Ed.), *Handbook of research on curriculum* (pp. 3–40). Macmillan.

Johnson, M. (1967). Definitions and models in curriculum theory. *Educational Theory, 17*(2), 127–140.

Johnson, M. (1969). The translation of curriculum into instruction. *Journal of Curriculum Studies, 1*(2), 115–131.

Johnson, M. (1977). *Intentionality in education: A conceptual model of curricular and instructional planning and evaluation*. Center for Curriculum Research and Services.

Jones, J. R. (2002). *A grammar of Christian faith*. Rowman & Littlefield.

Jonnaert, P., & Thevriault, G. (2013). Curricula and curriculum analysis: Some pointers for debate. *Prospects, 43*(4), 379–417.

Kemmis, S. (1995). Emancipatory aspirations in a postmodern era. *Curriculum Studies, 3*(2), 133–167. (The journal currently known as *Pedagogy, Culture and Society*.)

Kemmis, S. (2009). Understanding professional practice: A synoptic framework. In B. Green (Ed.), *Understanding and researching professional practice* (pp. 19–38). Sense.

Kemmis, S. (2010). What is professional practice? Recognizing and respecting diversity in understanding practice. In C. Kanes (Ed.), *Elaborating professionalism: Studies in practice and theory* (pp. 139–165). Springer.

Kemmis, S., Wilkinson, J., Edwards-Groves, C., Hardy, I., Grootenboer, P., & Bristol, L. (2014). *Changing practices, changing education*. Springer.

Kemp, G. (2018). *What is this thing called philosophy of language?* (3rd ed.). Routledge.

Kennedy, K. J. (1988). Creating a context for curriculum deliberation by teachers. ERIC Document Reproduction Service. ED 301 965.

Kennedy, K. J. (Ed.) (1990). *Case studies in curriculum design*. West Australian Social Science Education Consortium.

Kimpston, R. D., & Anderson, D. H. (1982). A study to analyze curriculum decision making in school districts. *Educational Leadership*, 40(2), 63–66.

Klein, M. F., & Goodlad, J. I. (1979). Curriculum development in cross-national perspective. In J. I. Goodlad & associates, *Curriculum inquiry: The study of curriculum practice* (pp. 259–285). McGraw-Hill.

Knapp, M., & Hopmann, S. T. (2017). School leadership as gap management: Curriculum traditions, changing evaluation parameters, and school leadership pathways. In M. Uljens, & R. M. Ylimaki (Eds.), *Bridging educational leadership, curriculum theory and Didaktik* (pp. 229–256). Springer.

Knitter, W. (1985). Curriculum deliberation: Pluralism and the practical. *Journal of Curriculum Studies*, 17(4), 383–395.

Kotarbinski, T. (1965). *Praxilology: An introduction to the sciences of efficient action*. Pergamon Press.

Kuiper, W., Nieveen, N., & Visscher-Voerman, I. (2003). Curriculum development from a technical-professional perspective. In J. van den Akker, W. Kuiper, & U. Hameyer (Eds.), *Curriculum landscapes and trends* (pp. 177–198). Springer.

Lam, T. S. J. (2011). Deliberation and school-based curriculum development—A Hong Kong case study. *New Horizons in Education*, 59(2), 69–82.

Lamm, Z. (1969). Teaching and curriculum planning. *Journal of Curriculum Studies*, 1(2), 159–171.

Laska, J. A. (1984). The relationship between instruction and curriculum: A conceptual clarification. *Instructional Science*, 13(3), 203–212.

Lewis, A. J., & Miel, A. (1972). *Supervision for improved instruction: New challenges, new responses*. Wadsworth.

Macagnoni, V. M. (1970). Social Dimensions of the Self as an Open System: A Curriculum Design—Strategies for Implementation. *Research Bulletin (Florida Educational Research and Development Council)*, 5(4), 1–68.

Macdonald, J. B. (1965). Introduction. In J. B. Macdonald & R. R. Leeper (Eds.), *Theories of Instruction*. Association for Supervision and Curriculum Development.

Macdonald, J. B. (1977). Value bases and issues in curriculum. In A. Molnar & J. A. Zahorik (Eds.), *Curriculum theory* (pp. 10–21). Association for Supervision and Curriculum Development. Reprinted in B. J. Macdonald (Ed.) (1995). *Theory as a prayerful act: The collected essays of James B. Macdonald* (pp. 137–148). Peter Lang.

Macdonald, J. B. (1986). The domain of curriculum. *Journal of Curriculum and Supervision*, 1(3), 205–214.

Macdonald, J. B., & Purpel, D. E. (1987). Curriculum and planning: Visions and metaphors. *Journal of Curriculum and Supervision*, 2(2), 178–192.

MacIntyre, A. (1984). *After virtue* (2nd ed.). Notre Dame University Press.

Macmillan, C. J. B., & Nelson, T. W. (Eds.) (1968). *Concepts of teaching*. Rand McNally.

Mahon, K., Kemmis, S., & Francisco, S., & Lloyd, A. (2017). Introduction: Practice theory and the theory of practice architectures. In K. Mahon, S. Francisco, & S. Kemmis (Eds.), *Exploring education and professional practice* (pp. 1–10). Springer.

Markauskaite, L., & Goodyear, P. (2014). Professional work and knowledge. In S. Billett, C. Harteis, & H. Gruber (Eds.), *International handbook of research in professional and practice-based learning* (pp. 79–106). Springer.

Marsh, C. J., Day, C., Hannay, L, & McCutcheon, G. (1990). *Reconceptualizing school-based curriculum development*. Falmer.

Marsh, C. J., & Willis, G. (2007). *Curriculum: Alternative approaches, ongoing issues* (4th ed.). Pearson Merrill.

Marshall, J. D., Sears, J. T., & Schubert, W. H. (2000). *Turning points in curriculum: A contemporary American memoir*. Merrill.

McClure, R. M. (1979). Institutional decisions in curriculum. In J. I. Goodlad & associates, *Curriculum inquiry: The study of curriculum practice* (pp. 129–150). McGraw-Hill.

McCutcheon, G. (1995). *Developing the curriculum: Solo and group deliberation*. Longman.

McKeon, R. (1952). Philosophy and action, *Ethics*, 62(2), 79–100.

McPhail, G. J. (2016). From aspiration to practice: Curriculum challenges for a new twenty-first century secondary school. *The Curriculum Journal*, 27(4), 518–537.

Mfum-Mensah, O. (2009). An exploratory study of the curriculum development process of a complementary education program for marginalized communities in Northern Ghana. *Curriculum Inquiry, 39*(2), 343–367.

Mitchell, W. J. T. (1981). *On narrative*. University of Chicago Press.

Molstad, C. E. (2015). State-based curriculum-making: Approaches to local curriculum work in Norway and Finland. *Journal of Curriculum Studies, 47*(4), 441–461.

Morris, C. W. (1938). *Foundations of the theory of signs: International encyclopedia of unified science*. Vol. 1, no. 2. University of Chicago Press.

Mulder, M. (1991). Deliberation in curriculum conferences. *Journal of Curriculum and Supervision, 6*(4), 325–339.

Mulder, M. (1994). Deliberation in curriculum conferences. In J. T. Dillon (Ed.), *Deliberation in education and society* (pp. 157–209). Ablex.

Myers, D. A. (1970). *Decision making in curriculum & instruction*. Institute for Development of Educational Activities.

Nadler, G. (1981). *The planning and design approach*. John Wiley & Sons.

Noye, D. (1994). Guidelines for conducting deliberations. In J. T. Dillon (Ed.), *Deliberation in education and society* (pp. 239–248). Ablex.

Oliver, A. I. (1977). *Curriculum improvement: A guide to problems, principles, and process* (2nd ed.). Harper & Row.

Orpwood, G. W. F. (1985). The reflective deliberator: A case study of curriculum policymaking. *Journal of Curriculum Studies, 17*(3), 293–304.

Parker, D. H. (1926). *The analysis of art*. Yale University Press.

Parsons, T. (1968). Professions. In D. L. Shils (Ed.), *International encyclopedia of the social sciences* (vol. 12, pp. 536–547). Macmillan.

Parsons, T., & Shils, E. A. (Eds.) (1951). *Toward a general theory of action*. Harvard University Press.

Pereira, P. (1984). Deliberation and the arts of perception. *Journal of Curriculum Studies, 16*(4), 347–366.

Phenix, P. H. (1964). Esthetics. In *Realms of meaning* (pp. 139–144). McGraw-Hill.

Polakow, V. (1986). On meaning making and stories: Young children's experiences with texts. *Phenomenology + Pedagogy, 4*(3), 37–47.

Polkinghorne, D. E. (1988). *Narrative knowing and the human sciences*. State University of New York Press.

Polkinghorne, D. E. (2004). *Practice and the human sciences: The case for a judgment-based practice of care*. State University of New York Press.

Portelli, J. P. (1987). On defining curriculum. *Journal of Curriculum and Supervision*, 2(4), 354–367.

Posner, G. J. (1992/2004). *Analyzing the curriculum*. McGraw Hill.

Priestley, M., & Philipou, S. (2018). Curriculum making as social practice: Complex webs of enactment. *Curriculum Journal*, 29(2), 151–158.

Pring, R. (1975). The language of curriculum analysis. In P. Hirst, et al. (Eds.), *The curriculum* (pp. 54–69). University of London, Institute of Education. Reprinted in R. Pring (2004). *Philosophy of education: Aims, theory, common sense, and research* (2nd ed.) (pp. 163–179). Continuum.

Raup, R. B., Axtelle, G. E., Benne, K. D., & Smith, B. O. (1962). *The improvement of practical intelligence: The central task of education* (rev. ed.). Bureau of Publications, Teachers College, Columbia University.

Reid, W. A. (1975). The changing curriculum: Theory and practice. In W. A. Reid & D. F. Walker (Eds.), *Case studies in curriculum change: Great Britain and the United States* (pp. 240–259). Routledge & Kagan Paul.

Reid, W. A. (1978/2013). *Thinking about the curriculum: The nature and treatment of curriculum problems*. Routledge.

Reid, W. A. (1988). The institutional context of curriculum deliberation. *Journal of Curriculum and Supervision*, 4(1), 3–16.

Reid, W. A. (1999). *Curriculum as institution and practice: Essays in the deliberative tradition*. Lawrence Erlbaum.

Robinson, R. (1972). *Definition*. Clarendon Press.

Roby, T. W. (1985). Habits impeding deliberation. *Journal of Curriculum Studies*, 17(1), 17–35.

Rosenmund, M. (2002). Approaches to international comparative research on curricula and curriculum-making processes. In M. Rosenmund, A. Fries, & W. Heller (Eds.), *Comparing curriculum-making processes* (pp. 289–300). Peter Lang.

Rugg, H., et al. (1927). *Curriculum-making: Past and present*. 26th Yearbook of National Society for the Study of Education, Part 1. Public School Publishing Company.

Ruzgar, M. E. (2018). On matters that matter in curriculum studies: an interview with Ian Westbury. *Journal of Curriculum Studies*, 50(6), 670–684,

Saylor, J. G., & Alexander, W. M. (1966). *Curriculum planning for modern schools.* (2nd ed.). Holt, Rinehart and Winston.

Schaffarzick, J. (1975). Questions and requirements for comparative study of curriculum development. In J. Schaffarzick & D. H. Hampson (Eds.), *Strategies for curriculum development* (pp. 211–256). McCutchan.

Schatzki, T. R. (1996). *Social practices: A Wittgensteinian approach to human activity and the social.* Cambridge University Press.

Schatzki, T. R. (2001). Introduction: Practice theory. In T. R. Schatzki, K. Knorr-Cetina, & E. van Savigny (Eds.), *The practice turn in contemporary theory* (pp. 1–14). Routledge.

Schatzki, T. R. (2012). A primer on practices. In J. Higgs, R. Barnett, S. Billett, M. Hutchings, & F. Trede (Eds.), *Practice-based education: Perspectives and strategies* (pp. 13–26). Sense.

Schatzki, T. R. (2018). On practice theory, or what's practices got to do with it? In C. Edwards-Groves, P. Grootenboer, & J. Wilkinson (Eds.), *Education in an era of schooling* (pp. 151–165). Springer.

Schubert, W. H. (1980). Recalibrating educational research: Toward a focus on practice. *Educational Researcher, 9*(1), 17–24, 31.

Schubert, W. H. (1986). Curriculum research controversy: A special case of a general problem. *Journal of Curriculum and Supervision, 1*(2), 132–147.

Schwab, J. J. (1969). The practical: A language for curriculum. *School Review, 78*(1), 1–23.

Schwab, J. J. (1973). The practical: Translation into curriculum. *School Review, 81*(4), 501–522.

Schwab, J. J. (1983). The practical 4: Something for curriculum professors to do. *Curriculum Inquiry, 13*(3), 239–265.

Schwandt, T. A. (2005). On modeling our understanding of the practice fields. *Pedagogy, Culture and Society, 13*(3), 313–332.

Schwyzer, H. (1969). Rules and practices. *Philosophical Review, 78*(4), 451–467.

Searle, J. R. (1970). *Speech acts: An essay in the philosophy of language.* Cambridge University Press.

Sears, J. T. (2004). The curriculum worker as public moral intellectual. In R. A. Gaztambide-Fernandez & J. T. Sears (Eds.), *Curriculum work as a public moral enterprise* (pp. 1–13). Rowman & Littlefield.

Shkedi, A. (1996). School-based workshops for teacher participation in curriculum development. *Journal of Curriculum Studies, 28*(6), 699–711.

Short, E. C. (1983). The forms and use of alternative curriculum development strategies: Policy implications. *Curriculum Inquiry*, 13(1), 43–64.
Short, E. C. (1991). Curriculum practice. *Journal of Curriculum and Supervision*, 6(4), 359–360.
Short, E. C. (2020) *A coherent curriculum for every student: Curriculum proposals for possible adoption*. Rowman & Littlefield.
Short, E. C. (2021, March 25). Curriculum proposals. In *Oxford Research Encyclopedia of Education*. Oxford University Press. doi: https://doi.org/10.1093/acrefore/9780190264093.013.1500
Siegel, J. E. (1977). Task No. 1: Writing 'practical' curriculums, *Educational Leadership*, 34(7), 540–544.
Skilbeck, M. (1982). School-based curriculum development. In V. Lee & D. Zeldin (Eds.), *Planning in the curriculum* (pp. 18–34). Hodder and Stoughton with Open University.
Skyttner, L. (2005). *General systems theory: Problems, perspectives, practice*. World Scientific.
Smith, B. O. (1963). A conceptual analysis of instructional behavior. *Journal of Teacher Education*, 14(3), 294–298.
Smith, B. O., Stanley, W. O., & Shores, J. H. (1950). *Fundamentals of curriculum development*. World Book.
Soltis, J. F. (1968). *An introduction to the analysis of educational concepts*. Addison-Wesley.
Steiner, E. (1978). *Logical and conceptual analysis techniques for educational researchers*. University Press of America.
Steiner, E. (1981). *Educology of the free*. Philosophical Library.
Steller, A. W. (1983). Curriculum planning. In F. English (Ed.), *Fundamental curriculum decisions* (pp. 68–89). Association for Supervision and Curriculum Development.
Stenhouse, L. (1975). *An introduction to curriculum research and development*. Heinemann.
Strike, K., & Posner, G. (1983). Types of synthesis and their criteria. In S. A. Ward & L. J. Reed (Eds.), *Knowledge structure and use: Implications for synthesis and interpretation* (pp. 345–362). Temple University Press.
Surbhi, S. (2015). Difference between training and education. Key Difference. https://keydifferences.com/difference-between-training-and-education.html
Taba, H. (1962). *Curriculum development: Theory and practice*. Harcourt, Brace, & World.

Tanner, D., & Tanner, L. (2007). *Curriculum development: Theory into practice* (4th ed.). Merrill Prentice Hall.

Thijs, A., & van den Akker, J. (Eds.). (2009). *Curriculum in development*. Netherlands Institute for Curriculum Development (SLO).

Torres Torres, J. M. (1999). A phenomenological study of the hidden life of teams [Unpublished doctoral dissertation. University of Maryland].

Tyler, R. W. (1949). *Basic principles of curriculum and instruction*. University of Chicago Press.

Uljens, M., & Ylimaki, R. M. (2017). Didaktik, curriculum and educational leadership. In M. Uljens & R. M. Ylimaki (Eds.), *Bridging educational leadership, curriculum theory and Didaktik: Non-affirmative theory of education* (pp. 36–40). Springer.

Vallance, E. (1983). Curriculum as a field of practice. In F. W. English (Ed.), *Fundamental curriculum decisions* (pp. 154–164). Association for Supervision and Curriculum Development.

van den Akker, J. (2003). Curriculum perspectives: An introduction. In J. van den Akker, W. Kuiper, & U. Hameyer (Eds.), *Curriculum landscapes and trends* (pp. 1–10). Kluwer Academic Publishers.

van den Akker, J. (2010). Building bridges: How research may improve curriculum policies and classroom practices. In S. M. Stoney (Ed.), *Beyond Lisbon 2010: Perspectives from research and development for education policy in Europe* (pp. 175–195). Consortium of Institutions for Development and Research in Education in Europe.

van den Akker, J. (2013). A European perspective on curriculum development and innovation. In E. H. Law & C. Li (Eds.), *Curriculum innovations in changing societies: Chinese perspectives from Hong Kong, Taiwan, and Mainland China* (pp. 535–545). Sense.

van Manen, M. (1977). Linking ways of knowing with ways of being practical. *Curriculum Inquiry*, 6(3), 205–228.

van Manen, M. (1999). Knowledge, reflection and complexity in teacher practice. In M. Lang, J. Olson, H. Hansen, & W. Bunder (Eds.), *Changing schools/changing practices* (pp. 65–75). Garant.

van Manen, M. (2007). Phenomenology of practice. *Phenomenology and Practice*, 1(1), 11–30.

van Manen, M. (2014). *Phenomenology of practice*. Left Coast Press.

Visscher-Voerman, J. I. A. (1999). Educational design and development: A study of Dutch design practices. In J. van den Akker, R. M. Branch, K. Gustafson, N. Nieveen, & T. Plomp (Eds.), *Design approaches and tools in education and training* (pp. 45–58). Kluwer.

Walker, D. F. (1971). A naturalistic model for curriculum development. *School Review*, 80(1), 51–65.
Walker, D. F. (1975). Curriculum development in an art project. In W. A. Reid & D. F. Walker (Eds.), *Case studies in curriculum change: Great Britain and the United States* (pp. 91–135). Routledge & Kagan Paul.
Walker, D. F. (1979). Approaches to curriculum development. In J. Schaffarzick & G. Sykes (Eds.), *Value conflicts and curriculum issues: Lessons from research and experience* (pp. 263–290). McCutchan.
Walker, D. F. (1992). Methodological issues in curriculum research. In P. W. Jackson (Ed.), *Handbook of research on curriculum* (pp. 98–118). Macmillan.
Walker, D. F. (2003). *Fundamentals of curriculum* (2nd ed.). Lawrence Erlbaum.
Westbury, I. (1972). The character of a curriculum for a "practical" curriculum. *Curriculum Theory Network*, (10), 25–36.
Westbury, I. (2008). Making curriculum: Why do states make curriculum, and how? In F. M. Connelly, M. F. He, & J. Phillion (Eds.), *The Sage handbook of curriculum and instruction* (pp. 45–65). Sage.
Whitson, J. A. (2009). Is there no outside of curriculum-as-text? In E. Ropo & T. Autio (Eds.), *International conversations on curriculum studies: Subject, society, and curriculum* (pp. 339–354). Sense.
Wilson, E. C. (1979). Designing institutional curricula: A case study of curriculum practice. In J. I. Goodlad & associates, *Curriculum inquiry: The study of curriculum practice* (pp. 209–239). McGraw-Hill.
Wise, R. J. (1979). The need for retrospective accounts of curriculum development. *Journal of Curriculum Studies*, 11(1), 17–28.
Wittgenstein, L. (1968). *Philosophical investigations* (3rd ed.). Macmillan.
Wraga, W. G. (2006). Curriculum theory and development and public policy making, *Journal of Curriculum and Pedagogy*, 3(1), 83–87.
Yinger, R. J. (1987). Learning the language of practice. *Curriculum Inquiry*, 17(3), 283–318.
Young, J. H. (1979). Teacher participation in curriculum decision-making: An organizational dilemma. *Curriculum Inquiry*, 9(2), 113–127.
Zais, R. S. (1976). *Curriculum: Principles and foundations*. Harper & Row.

Index

Page numbers in italics denote figures; those with a *t* indicate tables; those with an *n* indicate notes.

administrative arrangements for curriculum, 38–39, 42t, 81t, 125n2
Anderson, D. H., 53
Aristotle, 123n2
assumptive component of curriculum, 32–33, 41t, 80t
Austin, J. L., 78, 87

Beauchamp, G. A., 10t, 26t
Ben-Peretz, M., 54
Berman, L. M., 10t
Bertalanffy, L., 10t
Biesta, G. J., 20, 52
Boersma, K., 54
Bourdieu, Pierre, 14
Broudy, H. S., 16–17

Carr, D., 10t
Chen, D., 54
Christiansen, J. E., 20
Clandinin, D. J., 10–11t
conceptions, 74–75
Connelly, F. M., 10–11t

content standards, 116
contextual realities component of curriculum, 32–35, 41t, 80t
Coombs, J. R., 17
curriculum: components of, 24 45, 26–28t, 41–42t, 43, 80–81t; conceptualizations of, 22–24, 23t, 48–54; core, 34; definitions of, 15–19, 44–45; design/development of, 7–8, 10t, 49–54, 58–59, 106–107; didactic, 20; evaluation of, 37–38, 42t, 43, 81t, 116; key concepts of, 49–52; long-range goals of, 28t, 30; similar terms to, 19–20; teaching and, 2–3, 19–21, 108–109; terminology of, 2
curriculum practice, 2–4. *See also* grammar of curriculum practice; conceptual classifications of, 55–56t, 55–62; definitions of, 5–14, 47–48, 84–86, 89, 91, 105;

curriculum practice (*continued*)
deliberations over, 56t, 61–72, 67–68t, 109; enactment guidelines for, 60–61; expertise in, 60; key concepts of, 52–54; "logic" of, 124n1; perspectives on, 10–11t; prescriptive statements of, 76–78; scholarly literature on, 2–3, 7–8, 126n2; Schwab on, 62–63; training for, 125n1

Daniels, L. B., 17
de Saussure, Ferdinand, 87
decision making, 55t, 56–57, 69–70, 72–75
deliberations, 56t; action-related, 69, 93, 97–98, 102–103; Aristotle on, 123n2; curriculum practice with, 61–72, 67–68t, 83–84, 106–107, 109; definitions of, 63–64, 69, 93; objects of, 72; practicality of, 93–94; Walker on, 50, 64, 66, 67t, 68t
Derr, R. L., 17
Dillon, J. T., 66, 68t
directives, 78–79, 80–81t, 82–83, 103; construction of, 94–96; promulgation of, 107; structure of, 96–97
discipline-centered organization, 34
doctrines, 82, 83, 103–104
Doyle, W., 26t
Duncan, J. K., 17, 26t

Eash, M. J., 26t

efficiency, 10t
Egan, Kieran, 20
Eible, C. V., 53
Eisner, E. W, 8, 11t, 12, 17, 50
Eraut, M., 51
evaluation of curriculum, 37–38, 42t, 43, 81t, 116

Faix, T. L., 10t, 16
Fisher, J. E., 20
fittingness, 94, 97–98
fixed procedures, 55t, 57
formulating directives for thought and action, 94
Foshay, A. W., 26t
Frymier, J. R., 17, 26t

Gagne, R. M., 20
Gay, G., 51
Goodlad, J. I., 10t, 26t, 50, 53
Goodyear, P., 10t
grammar of curriculum practice, 1, 87–88, 110–11. *See also* curriculum practice; analysis of, 121n1; assumptions of, 88–89; conceptualization of, 87–99, 100–101t, 112–14; definitions of, 89, 98, 102–104; implications of, 125n1; language of, 90–91; value of, 105–12
Green, Bill, 123n4

Harris, I. B., 65–66, 68t, 76–77, 82
Heidegger, Martin, 10t
Herrick, V. E., 7, 9, 26t, 49
Hopmann, S. T., 20

Huebner, D. E., 7, 9, 16, 26t

instruction, 20–21. See also teaching

integrated curriculum, 34

intentional component of curriculum, 31–32, 41t, 80t

Iwanska, A., 10t

Johnson, M., 20, 26t, 49

Jones, J. R., 6, 9, 87–88

justification component of curriculum, 39–40, 42t, 81t

Kemmis, S., 7, 9, 10t, 14

Kemp, G., 87

Kimpston, R. D., 53

Klein, M. F., 53

Knapp, M., 20

knowledge acquisition, 10t

Kotarbinski, T., 10t

language communities, 88

learning, defined, 20

learning practices, 125n1

Looy, F., 54

Macdonald, J. B., 9, 10t, 26t, 51, X7

MacIntyre, A., 6, 9, 10t

Macmillan, C. J. B., 20

Mahon, K., 14, 105

Markauskaite, L., 10t

Marsh, C. J., 51

McCutcheon, G., 66, 68t

Morris, C. W., 87

Nadler, G., 10t

negotiating consensus, 55t, 59–60

Nelson, T. W., 20

noncontradiction principle, 93, 95–97

Noye, D., 66, 68t

organizational component of curriculum, 35–36, 41t, 80t

Orpwood, G. W. F., 54, 65, 67t

Parsons, T., 10t

Pereira, P., 65, 67t

Polakow, V., 10t

Polkinghorne, D. E., 14

Posner, G. J., 27t

practical reasoning, 55t, 64, 93–94

practice, 10–11t. See also curriculum practice; definitions of, 5–7, 12–14, 47, 105

pragmatics, 88, 89

preferred conceptions, 72–75

Prescribed Action Plan, 22–24, 37, 40, 91

prescribed curriculum plan, 83, 91–92, 94

prescriptive statements, 76–77, 82–84, 97

problem-solving strategies, 55t, 57–58

professionalism, 10t

Purpel, D. E., 10t, 51

Reid, W. A., 50, 64, 67t

Saussure, Ferdinand de, 87

Schatski, T. R., 7, 9, 13

Schubert, W. H., 26t
Schwab, J. J., 8, 11t, 12; on
 curriculum, 17, 49–50; on
 deliberation, 64–65, 67t
Schwandt, T. A., 6, 9
Searle, J. R., 87
semantics, 88, 91, 94–97
Shils, E. A., 10t
Skilbeck, M., 50
Skyttner, L., 10t
Smith, B. O., 20
Soltis, J. F., 20
Steiner, E., 20
Steller, A. W., 50–51
Stengel, B. S., 20
Stenhouse, L., 17
student transactive component
 of curriculum, 36, 41t, 81t
substantive component of
 curriculum, 29–31, 33, 41t,
 80t
supportive arrangements of
 curriculum, 38–39, 42t, 81t,
 125n2
Surbhi, S., 20
syntax, 87–88

Taba, H., 10t, 49
Tamir, P., 54

Tanner, D., 18, 51
Tanner, L., 18, 51
teaching: curriculum and, 2–3,
 19–21, 108–109; definitions of,
 20–21; practice of, 3; training
 for, 21; transactive component
 of, 36–37, 41t, 81t
Tyler, R. W., 10t, 49

Uljens, M., 8, 12

van den Akker, J., 10t, 27t, 52
van Manen, M., 10t
Visscher-Voerman, J. I. A., 54

Walker, D. F., 7–9, 11t, 12;
 on curriculum, 18; on
 deliberations, 50, 64, 66, 67t,
 68t
Westbury, I., 51–52
Willis, G., 51
Wilson, E. C., 53
Wise, R. J., 8, 9
Wittgenstein, Ludwig, 87

Ylimaki, R. M., 8, 12

Zais, R. S., 26t
Zavarella, J. A., 53

About the Author

Edmund C. Short is professor Emeritus of Education at The Pennsylvania State University, and currently graduate faculty associate at College of Community Innovation and Education, University of Central Florida. He received his EdD from Teachers College, Columbia University, and has held faculty positions at Ball State University, University of Toledo, The Pennsylvania State University, Georgia Southern University, and University of Central Florida. His academic and professional activities have focused primarily on development, research, and theory in the field of curriculum practice. He has written numerous articles on these subjects in leading journals, handbooks, and encyclopedias. His most widely known books include *Forms of Curriculum Inquiry; Leaders in Curriculum Studies: Intellectual Self-Portraits;* and *A Coherent Curriculum for Every Student: Curriculum Proposals for Possible Adoption.* He may be contacted at edcoshort@gmail.com.

www.ingramcontent.com/pod-product-compliance
Lightning Source LLC
Chambersburg PA
CBHW030828230426
43667CB00008B/1428